PHILIPPIANS

REFORMED EXPOSITORY BIBLE STUDIES

A Companion Series to the Reformed Expository Commentaries

Series Editors

Daniel M. Doriani
Iain M. Duguid
Richard D. Phillips
Philip Graham Ryken

1 Samuel: A King after God's Own Heart
Esther & Ruth: The Lord Delivers and Redeems
Song of Songs: Friendship on Fire
Daniel: Faith Enduring through Adversity
Matthew: Making Disciples for the Nations (two volumes)
Luke: Knowing for Sure (two volumes)
Galatians: The Gospel of Free Grace
Ephesians: The Glory of Christ in the Life of the Church
Philippians: To Live Is Christ
Hebrews: Standing Firm in Christ
James: Portrait of a Living Faith

Forthcoming

John: The Word Incarnate (two volumes)

PHILIPPIANS

TO LIVE IS CHRIST

A 13-LESSON STUDY

REFORMED EXPOSITORY
BIBLE STUDY

JON NIELSON
and **DENNIS E. JOHNSON**

P&R
PUBLISHING
P.O. BOX 817 • PHILLIPSBURG • NEW JERSEY 08865-0817

ISBN: 978-1-62995-924-5 (pbk)
ISBN: 978-1-62995-925-2 (ePub)

CONTENTS

SERIES INTRODUCTION

Studying the Bible will change your life. This is the consistent witness of Scripture and the experience of people all over the world, in every period of church history.

King David said, "The law of the LORD is perfect, reviving the soul; the testimony of the LORD is sure, making wise the simple; the precepts of the LORD are right, rejoicing the heart; the commandment of the LORD is pure, enlightening the eyes" (Ps. 19:7–8). So anyone who wants to be wiser and happier, and who wants to feel more alive, with a clearer perception of spiritual reality, should study the Scriptures.

Whether we study the Bible alone or with other Christians, it will change us from the inside out. The Reformed Expository Bible Studies provide tools for biblical transformation. Written as a companion to the Reformed Expository Commentary, this series of short books for personal or group study is designed to help people study the Bible for themselves, understand its message, and then apply its truths to daily life.

Each Bible study is introduced by a pastor-scholar who has written a full-length expository commentary on the same book of the Bible. The individual chapters start with the summary of a Bible passage, explaining **The Big Picture** of this portion of God's Word. Then the questions in **Getting Started** introduce one or two of the passage's main themes in ways that connect to life experience. These questions may be especially helpful for group leaders in generating lively conversation.

Understanding the Bible's message starts with seeing what is actually there, which is where **Observing the Text** comes in. Then the Bible study provides a longer and more in-depth set of questions entitled **Understanding the Text**. These questions carefully guide students through the entire passage, verse by verse or section by section.

It is important not to read a Bible passage in isolation, but to see it in the wider context of Scripture. So each Bible study includes two **Bible Connections** questions that invite readers to investigate passages from other places in Scripture—passages that add important background, offer valuable contrasts or comparisons, and especially connect the main passage to the person and work of Jesus Christ.

The next section is one of the most distinctive features of the Reformed Expository Bible Studies. The authors believe that the Bible teaches important doctrines of the Christian faith, and that reading biblical literature is enhanced when we know something about its underlying theology. The questions in **Theology Connections** identify some of these doctrines by bringing the Bible passage into conversation with creeds and confessions from the Reformed tradition, as well as with learned theologians of the church.

Our aim in all of this is to help ordinary Christians apply biblical truth to daily life. **Applying the Text** uses open-ended questions to get people thinking about sins that need to be confessed, attitudes that need to change, and areas of new obedience that need to come alive by the power and influence of the Holy Spirit. Finally, each study ends with a **Prayer Prompt** that invites Bible students to respond to what they are learning with petitions for God's help and words of praise and gratitude.

You will notice boxed quotations throughout the Bible study. These quotations come from one of the volumes in the Reformed Expository Commentary. Although the Bible study can stand alone and includes everything you need for a life-changing encounter with a book of the Bible, it is also intended to serve as a companion to a full commentary on the same biblical book. Reading the full commentary is especially useful for teachers who want to help their students answer the questions in the Bible study at a deeper level, as well as for students who wish to further enrich their own biblical understanding.

The people who worked together to produce this series of Bible studies have prayed that they will engage you more intimately with Scripture, producing the kind of spiritual transformation that only the Bible can bring.

Philip Graham Ryken
Coeditor of the Reformed Expository Commentary series

INTRODUCING PHILIPPIANS

The epistle to the Philippians is a frank and encouraging pastoral letter from the apostle Paul to a congregation that he loves (see Phil. 4:1). His aims for this epistle are accomplished at two levels. At one level, Paul is writing to thank the Philippians for a generous contribution they have made toward his expenses (see 1:5; 4:10–20). Moreover, concern that the Philippians have shown over his well-being and over a health crisis that has been suffered by their representative, Epaphroditus, prompts Paul to reassure them (see 1:12–18; 2:25–30).

At a deeper level, however, the thank-you note Paul is writing gives him an opportunity to pursue a greater **main purpose**: that of addressing the congregation's underlying spiritual needs. He is suffering opposition, and so are they; and the joyful perspective that he takes on suffering—that its function is to advance Christ's gospel—invites his Philippian friends to see their experience in a new light and to replace cowardice with courage. After describing the "selfish ambition" of some who preach Christ in order to compound Paul's pain (see 1:16–17), the apostle warns his dear friends against the "selfish ambition" that undermines their own unity (see 2:1–4). The negative influence that self-righteous legalists are having on the church then moves Paul to rehearse the transition he himself made away from boasting in his own credentials in order to instead gratefully trust in Christ and his righteousness (see 3:2–9). Paul also lifts his friends' sights to heaven, where their citizenship is held and from where they await their Savior's return (see 3:12–21). Finally, Paul turns his thanks for the Philippians' generosity into a teaching moment about Christ-centered contentment (see 4:10–19).

This epistle's **author** is Paul the apostle (see 1:1), who once persecuted Christ's church (see 3:4–6). Since Paul's apostolic authority is accepted in Philippi, Paul bypasses the title "apostle" and identifies himself and Timothy

9

as "servants" of Christ Jesus. His use of the word *servants* is strategic, for Paul goes on to urge his friends to exhibit the mind of Christ, who humbly took "the form of a servant" for the sake of their salvation (2:7).

The epistle's **audience** is "all the saints in Christ Jesus who are at Philippi, with the overseers and deacons" (1:1). Acts 16:11–40 records how this church was planted in Philippi, "a leading city of . . . Macedonia" (v. 12), by Paul and Silas, whose team included Timothy (see vv. 1–3) as well as Luke, the author of Acts (see v. 11). Apparently the missionaries found no Jewish synagogue in Philippi, so their search for people who were worshipping the true God of Israel led them to a "place of prayer" by a river outside the city (v. 13). This absence of a synagogue in the city suggests that its Jewish community was so small that it lacked the minimum of ten Jewish men who were necessary for forming one.

All evidence points to the Philippian congregation's being overwhelmingly composed of Gentiles—which would be consistent with Paul's distinctive calling as apostle to the Gentiles (see Rom. 11:13; Gal. 2:7–9). Luke's account of the trip to Philippi focuses on three individuals whose lives were transformed by Christ's power: Lydia, a textile importer from Thyatira who was a Gentile adherent to Israel's faith (see Acts 16:13–15); a demon-possessed slave who was being exploited by her owners for her (alleged) ability for fortune-telling (see vv. 16–18); and a jailer who was converted along with his family (see vv. 25–34). We know that by the time Paul and his missionary team left Philippi, a fledgling congregation had formed there, since we see other "brothers" gathered at Lydia's home to bid them farewell in verse 40. Paul reminds his friends, in Philippians 1:30, that they had witnessed the unjust treatment he and Silas had suffered when they had brought Christ's good news to Philippi (see Acts 16:22–24, 36–39).

As Paul writes this epistle, roughly a decade later, the congregation has matured and now has a plurality of overseers (that is, "elders"—Acts 14:23) and deacons. The bonds of affection between Paul and this congregation have deepened through the ongoing tangible care they have shown him. As Paul was ministering in Thessalonica, Athens, and Corinth, the Christians of Philippi—who were not affluent (see 2 Cor. 8:2)—repeatedly provided financial support for his ministry (see 2 Cor. 11:8–9; Phil. 4:10–19). Nor was their generosity limited to a monetary transaction: "They gave themselves first to the Lord and then by the will of God to us" (2 Cor. 8:5). It is no wonder, then, that Paul gives the Philippians the assurance that "I hold you in my heart. . . . I yearn for you all with the affection of Christ Jesus" (Phil. 1:7–8).

Although they are free of many of the grave spiritual crises that Paul has had to address in other churches, the Philippian congregation nonetheless faces challenges that require pastoral intervention. Paul mentions the opponents who are confronting them and the suffering they are enduring (see 1:28–30) as he urges them to stand firm and united (see v. 27). His summons to them to be unified and to focus on others' interests instead of their own suggests that "selfish ambition" and "conceit" have been threatening these believers' unity (see 2:1–4)—a suggestion that he confirms when he later appeals to two women in the congregation to "agree in the Lord" (see 4:2–3). Although the Philippians have not succumbed to the influence of Judaizing legalism or of reckless lawlessness, Paul still seeks to safeguard them from both (see 3:1–19).

Two **contexts** are significant to our study: both Paul's and the Philippian Christians'. Paul is in chains (see 1:13–17) and anticipating an event in which he wants to conduct himself with courage (see 1:19–20). The most widely held and reasonable theory is that Paul is writing from Rome, where he awaits the hearing of his appeal to the Roman emperor Nero (see Acts 28:11–31)—an appeal that could result in either his execution or his exoneration. Consistent with Roman legal practice, Paul is bearing his own living expenses while he is in custody (see v. 30), which made the donation the Philippians have given to him particularly welcome. He is seeking the prayerful support of his brothers and sisters so that he may acquit himself courageously as Christ's spokesman (see Phil. 1:19–20).

We explored some significant features of the Philippians' own context when we were considering them as the book's audience. One more aspect of their context that casts light on this epistle is the honored status that Philippi held as a Roman "colony" (Acts 16:12)—the citizens of which would enjoy the same privileges as did the citizens of Rome itself. As he writes to them, Paul draws from Philippi's status as a colony to assure Christians that their citizenship is in heaven—that their identity and status are defined by the city from which their Savior (a title that Romans applied to their Caesars) will return in glory (see Phil. 3:20–21). Therefore Paul directs them to acquit themselves in a way that is "worthy of the gospel of Christ" (1:27).

If a single **key verse** encapsulates the message of Philippians, it would be Philippians 1:21: "For to me to live is Christ, and to die is gain." In its immediate context, this statement is referring to the possible outcomes of Paul's hearing before Caesar: *ongoing life* on earth, so that he can serve Christ's people, or *death*—which would be "far better" for him, since he would then "be with Christ" (see 1:22–26). But his assertion that "to live is Christ" not only transforms our perspective on *suffering* but also applies to our *humility*, which preserves unity among Christians and leads us to serve others (see 2:1–11); to our *lifelong aspiration* to know Christ—to "gain Christ and be found in him" (see 3:4–11); and to our *contentment*, through thick and thin, which we find in "him who strengthens" us (4:13).

Two **theological themes** stand out in Philippians. First, Philippians 2:5–11 expresses, clearly and concisely, the whole New Testament's teaching concerning the *person of Christ*. He is fully God, and thus equal with the Father, and fully human—he humbles himself to die as Isaiah 53 foretells that the Suffering Servant will. Exalted by God as a reward for his redemptive self-sacrifice, Jesus Christ is the Lord of all, to whom every knee will bow. Second, the spiritual autobiography Paul lays out in Philippians 3:2–11 clearly articulates the *doctrine of justification by grace alone through faith alone in Christ alone*, which he has already explained at length in his epistles to the Galatians and to the Romans. Here Paul makes clear that, when he speaks of the "works of the law" (Gal. 2:16), he has in view not only the external covenant boundary markers that he once considered "gain" but also *anything in himself or his behavior* that once gave him "confidence in the flesh" (see Phil. 3:4–7)—any "righteousness of [his] own" that stands in contrast to "the righteousness from God that depends on faith" and that "comes through faith in Christ" (3:9). Christ's righteousness, alone, is the ground of justification, and we receive it through faith alone. Moreover, Paul shows that this faith that rests wholly in Christ's righteousness, far from fostering spiritual complacency, energizes believers to "press on" in order to know Christ more fully and so to receive "the prize of the upward call of God in Christ Jesus" (see 3:12–14). Justification, which we receive as God's free gift in Christ, fires our desire for and sustains our pursuit of holiness.

In terms of **practical application**, the first thing for us to notice is that Paul lays out these theological themes not as "entries" in a theological encyclopedia but as *truths that transform* our lives and relationships. In

2:5–11, Paul gives us the magnificent *carmen Christi* ("song of Christ") in order to support his appeal for his Philippian friends to "do nothing from selfish ambition or conceit, but in humility count others more significant than yourselves" (2:3). Likewise, Paul narrates the personal trajectory he followed from self-confidence to trust in Christ. He does so in order to protect his beloved sisters and brothers from the spiritual peril that is posed by righteous-looking, fine-sounding teachers who are, in reality, "dogs," "evildoers," and flesh mutilators (3:2). Nothing can be more practical than accurately drawing the line between theological truth and error. Along with every practical issue that he addresses in this brief epistle—our response to suffering, our choice between self-interest or concern for others, our confidence before God and hope for the future, our contentment no matter our circumstances—Paul repeatedly brings us back to *the touchstone of Christ* and the union we have with him by grace through our faith. As you study Philippians, notice that Christ centeredness!

Philippians shows us Paul's pastoral strategy of *teaching by example*. He devotes considerable space to writing about his imprisonment in order to model for suffering saints how they can respond to their own persecutors. He elaborates on his plans to send Timothy and Epaphroditus and hints that these leaders will show the Philippians what it looks like to seek others' interests (see 2:19–22; see also 2:1–4) and to risk one's life for the work of Christ (see 2:27–30). While he humbly acknowledges in 3:13 that he has not reached perfection, Paul still offers his mindset as one that the mature should share, and he even urges the whole congregation, "Join in imitating me, and keep your eyes on those who walk according to the example you have in us" (3:15-17). He does not reduce Christ's humility during his suffering to something merely exemplary—at its core, Christ's humble suffering is redemptive and substitutionary, as the echoes of Isaiah 53 in Philippians 2:5-11 demonstrate. Yet through our union with Christ we receive not only his imputed righteousness but also his "mind" (see 2:5), and "God . . . works in [us], both to will and to work for his good pleasure" (2:13).

Finally, by portraying for us a Christ-focused life, Paul is also inviting us to a life of invincible *joy*, no matter our challenges or circumstances. He rejoices when Christ is proclaimed—even by those who are motivated by rivalry instead of love (see 1:17–18). He rejoices at the prospect of reunions between fellow believers (see 1:25; 2:29). His joy is complete when Christians cultivate unity through their humility (see 2:1–4). His brothers and sisters in Jesus are his joy and his crown (see 4:1)—and so, of course, he prays for them with joy (see 1:4). Even if, instead of restoring Paul to his friends' company and giving him an opportunity to serve them further, Christ has ordained his imminent death, Paul rejoices over the possibility of being poured out on the sacrificial offering of their faith, and he urges them to share his joy (see 2:17–18). Jesus's Spirit has so saturated Paul's heart with deep joy, which springs not from changeable circumstances but from his changeless Lord, that the apostle urges his readers—not once, or twice, but three times—to

Rejoice in the Lord. (3:1)

Rejoice in the Lord always; again I will say, *rejoice*. (4:4)

OUTLINE

1. Introduction (1:1–11)
   A. Salutation (1:1–2)
   B. Thanksgiving and prayer (1:3–11)
2. Paul's Situation (1:12–26)
   A. Gospel advancement through chains (1:12–18)
   B. Life or death weighed against others' needs (1:19–26)
3. The Philippians' Situation (1:27–2:18)
   A. Unity in the face of external opponents (1:27–30)
   B. Humility toward each other (2:1–11)
   C. Purity amid a twisted generation (2:12–18)
4. Paul's Plans, and Some Trustworthy Examples (2:19–30)
5. The Twin Threats Facing the Philippian Church (3:1–21)
   A. Legalism versus rest in Christ's righteousness (3:1–16)
   B. Earthbound lawlessness versus heavenly citizenship (3:17–21)
6. Call to Staunch Unity, Joyful Prayer, and Pure Thought (4:1–9)
7. Partnership and Contentment (4:10–20)
8. Closing Greetings and Benediction (4:21–23)

Dennis E. Johnson
Author of *Philippians* (REC)

LESSON 1

FINISHING WHAT HE STARTS

Philippians 1:1–8

THE BIG PICTURE

Paul's epistle to the Philippians, which he most likely wrote while imprisoned in Rome, includes a rebuke of a local church congregation that was plagued by selfishness, disunity, and quarreling. Yet Paul practices his own instruction regarding thankful prayer, from Philippians 4:6, as he gives thanks for the believers in Philippi and exultantly assures them that God will continue the good work he has begun in them (1:6).

Paul's initial greeting introduces some key themes of the entire letter: he calls himself and Timothy "servants," or slaves, of Christ Jesus, which bespeaks Paul's humble understanding of the calling, ministry, and suffering he has experienced for Jesus and the gospel (1:1). The recipients of this letter are the "saints" in Philippi, which includes their leaders: the overseers and deacons. The fact that Paul addresses these leaders in particular, in verse 1, places some burden on these overseers of the church to respond to the calls from later in the epistle for both humility and unity to be promoted among God's people (v. 1). Finally, the blessing he pronounces of both "grace" and "peace" from God the Father and the Lord Jesus Christ speaks to the gospel foundation, and the relational implications, of all that he will go on to say to the church at Philippi (1:2).

After this greeting, Paul gives thanks for the believers at Philippi, who have boldly and generously partnered with him in gospel ministry for quite some time (1:3–5). Finally, he concludes with deeply personal words of affection for the dear brothers and sisters who have stood by him—even during his long imprisonment—and mentions his yearning to share fellowship with these gospel partners in person (1:7–8).

Read Philippians 1:1–8.

GETTING STARTED

1. Think of a time you saw a church struggle with disunity. What issues caused the problem? How did the church attempt to address them?

   Tusculm and the transition from Br. Doug to eventually Danny

2. Have you ever been tempted to doubt that God's saving work in your life will be completed? In what ways can sin, doubt, and weakness discourage you and tempt you to despair over your walk with Christ?

   It can make you doubt that God is actually hearing your prayers and worse answering them when you want, not how God wants.

The Antidote to Self-Centeredness, pg. 22

Paul's thanksgiving . . . reveals the heart of one who has received Christ's antidote to self-centeredness. Paul's thankful heart shows that as we entrust ourselves to Jesus, he gives two gifts: a love that stretches our hearts to embrace others, and a joy that places our pain into perspective, enabling us to see our suffering in the context of God's comprehensive plan to make us like his Son.

OBSERVING THE TEXT

3. What do you notice about the way Paul introduces himself at the outset of this letter? How does he describe his audience—and what does he emphasize and highlight about them?

4. List some of the reasons that Paul is thankful for the Philippian believers. How have they made their love for him—and for the gospel of Jesus Christ—clearly evident?

   - partnership in Gospel (financial support)
   - spiritual progress
   - Completion of the work

5. In these opening verses, what theological truths does Paul remind the Philippian church of in order to encourage them?

Joyful Slavery, pg. 8

The Philippians need to see dramatized in Paul and in Timothy the counterintuitive truth that these men bear God's *authority* because Christ has captivated them as his *slaves*. Paul and Timothy are living proof that those whom Jesus *saves* he *enslaves*. In their self-centered preoccupations and competing agendas, Paul's Philippian friends need to see what joyful slavery looks like, up close and personal.

UNDERSTANDING THE TEXT

6. Why do you think Paul uses the label *servant* (or *slave*) to describe
   Timothy and himself (1:1)? What themes does this label hint will be
   in this letter? What call does it hint that God has given to his people
   at Philippi?

   - To describe them as will ephis on service
     to Christ.

7. Why do you think Paul explicitly mentions "overseers and deacons" in
   his greeting (1:1)? What does his use of the label "saints" tell us about
   how he views the men and women in the church at Philippi?

8. What do you think Paul means when he mentions the Philippians'
   "partnership in the gospel" (1:5)? How might the Philippian church
   have been partnering with Paul (1:7)?

   Points to the working with the gospel
   and financial Support

9. Describe the assurance that Paul gives the Philippian believers in verse
   6—what "good work" is God going to complete, and what is the foundation for this good work?

   It is the continual faith that God
   will continue to do good works in
   my life until Jesus returns.

10. What emotions does Paul express regarding the Philippian believers in 1:7–8? What do they tell us about the apostle's relationships with the people and churches he served?

Partakers in grace awaiting the outcome of the appeal

11. What does Paul say in verses 5, 7, and 8 to emphasize the link and union he has with the Philippians? Even though they haven't been in prison with him or traveled and preached as he has, he sees them as collaborators in his gospel ministry—what does this illustrate for you about partnering in the gospel in our world today?

Partners. That they stood by Paul even when in Prison

BIBLE CONNECTIONS

12. Read Acts 16:11–34 to help you to recall the context of Paul's original gospel ministry in the city of Philippi. What notable conversions occurred during his visit? What resistance did his ministry face? What evidence of the power of the gospel do you see having occurred—even amid Paul's trials and suffering?

Signs of New Life, pg. 35
Are you trusting today in Jesus' blood and righteousness, rather than in your own achievements? That faith is the hallmark of those who have partnership in the gospel, who are partners with Paul in God's grace. Such trust is the sign of new life, showing that the living God has begun a good work in you, turning your ingrown heart "inside out," to adore him gratefully and to love others lavishly.

13. Read Ephesians 2:1–10, and note the *before* (vv. 1–3) and *after* (vv. 4–10) stages related to the gospel's work in our lives. How does this passage enhance our understanding of the "good work" that Philippians 1:6 says God has begun in all those who are saved by faith in Christ? What is God's purpose for his people?

THEOLOGY CONNECTIONS

14. The word *saints* (meaning "holy ones"), which Paul uses in Philippians 1:1 to describe the members of the church, illustrates the beautiful doctrine of the *priesthood of all believers*. In Christ, we are all holy—we have been declared righteous because of our faith in Jesus and given access to God the Father through him. How does this view of saints differ from that of other religious traditions or teachings?

15. The Westminster Confession of Faith describes sanctification with these words: "Sanctification is throughout, in the whole man, yet imperfect in this life, there abiding still some remnants of corruption in every part: whence arises a continual and irreconcilable war, the flesh lusting against the Spirit, and the Spirit against the flesh" (13.2). What does it mean that God's work in us will *never* be completed in this life? What will change at the "day of Jesus Christ" (Phil. 1:6)?

APPLYING THE TEXT

16. Paul's understanding that he is a "servant" or "slave" of Jesus Christ ought to shape our understanding of our own position before Jesus. What makes this a humbling position? Why is it also a freeing and empowering one?

17. What brothers and sisters in Christ would currently consider you to be a "partner" with them in the gospel—and why? How might you develop and increase your commitment to gospel ministry in your church or community?

18. What encouragement does Philippians 1:6 offer us? Why will it not work for us to use this verse to excuse a lack of spiritual effort, discipline, or desire for spiritual growth?

PRAYER PROMPT

As you conclude this first lesson in your study of Philippians, praise God for beginning a good work in you through the power of the Holy Spirit, who alone enables us to repent of our sin and have faith in Jesus Christ as our Savior and Lord. Thank him for the sovereign work he has done to accomplish your salvation and for the promise he has made to complete the work he has begun in you. Ask him for strength, energy, humility, and joy as you share in ministry with others who follow Jesus and proclaim the gospel.

LESSON 2

PRAYER AND PRISON

Philippians 1:9–18

THE BIG PICTURE

Paul's opening words of greeting and encouragement now give way to a beautiful prayer for the Philippian believers (1:9–11) in which he asks God to increase their love, knowledge, and discernment—and to ultimately make them blameless and pure on the day of Jesus Christ (v. 10). As do Paul's prayers in his other epistles, his petitions for the Philippian church demonstrate his deeply spiritual concerns for his audience—the apostle prays with eternity in view!

Next, Paul directs the Philippians' attention to his own situation—the imprisonment and affliction he is undergoing for the sake of the gospel (1:12–18). His purpose for highlighting his imprisonment is not so that he can elicit their pity, however; Paul longs for the Philippian believers to see how even his chains have contributed to the advancement of the gospel, because his witness has continued even while he has been in prison, which has emboldened others to preach without fear (vv. 12–14). Even though some people have used the opportunity of Paul's arrest to preach Christ from a competitive and envious spirit, Paul rejoices even in this—since it still means that the gospel is advancing forward (vv. 15–18).

Through both the prayer he offers for the Philippian church and the testimony he shares from *prison*, the apostle seeks to ground these believers' joy firmly in the eternal purposes of God as they await the day the Lord Jesus Christ returns.

Read Philippians 1:9–18.

GETTING STARTED

1. What kinds of things do people generally pray about the most, and why? What topics that the Bible tells us to pray about do we often overlook?

2. Why do the difficult or painful circumstances we experience sometimes hinder us from rejoicing with others who are experiencing blessing? Have you ever struggled to share someone else's joy because of your own pain? Why?

OBSERVING THE TEXT

3. In Philippians 1:9–11, Paul describes the prayers he offers to God on the Philippians' behalf. What kinds of requests does he make for them? What is the focus of these prayers?

A Model in Suffering, pgs. 55–56

[The Philippians] need to see in Paul, their father in the faith, how to handle the pain of persecution in a way that brings honor to their Lord and joy to their own hearts. Just as Paul opened his heart in his prayer report (1:9–11) to show the Philippians how to pray for one another, so his optimistic assessment of his situation models how they should evaluate their own difficulties.

4. What is surprising about the way Paul reacts to his imprisonment (1:12–14)? How might we expect someone to react to being imprisoned today?

5. How would you characterize Paul's tone throughout this passage? What attitude does he model for the Philippians? What perspective does he share with them regarding both his imprisonment and his rivals' preaching?

UNDERSTANDING THE TEXT

6. What specific areas of spiritual growth does Paul ask God to grant to the Philippians (1:9–10)? Why do you think Paul mentions these?

7. In what way do the day of judgment and the coming of Jesus Christ shape the prayers Paul offers for the Philippian church (1:10–11)?

8. How do you think the Philippians might have initially responded to hearing about Paul's imprisonment—and what better response does Paul demonstrate for them (1:12)?

9. What positive results—one regarding unbelievers and the other regarding believers—does Paul say have arisen from his imprisonment (1:13–14)?

10. What motivates Paul's rivals to preach the gospel while he is in prison (1:15–17)? What do these verses tell us about people's engagement in ministry and service?

11. Paul's reaction to those who are preaching the gospel from sinful and competitive motives is surprising as well (1:18)! What causes him to rejoice despite his affliction?

The Wellspring of Life, pg. 51
Jesus is the avenue through whom God will answer Paul's prayer for his friends. Jesus is the conduit through whom God pours overflowing love, with discerning wisdom, into their thirsty hearts. Jesus is the wellspring of life from whom they are absorbing nutrients that enable them to bear the fruit of peaceable righteousness.

BIBLE CONNECTIONS

12. Read Colossians 1:9–12, in which Paul tells the Colossian believers about the prayers he has been offering for them. What themes do you see in that prayer, and what requests does it contain, that are similar to those in the prayer we are studying from Philippians 1? Which of these details are different, between them, as a result of being unique to the specific churches he's writing to?

13. In Genesis 50:20, Joseph famously tells his brothers who had sold him as a slave, "You meant evil against me, but God meant it for good." In what ways is Paul's perspective similar to Joseph's? How does the death of Jesus Christ our Savior illustrate this same principle?

THEOLOGY CONNECTIONS

14. Answer 1 of the Westminster Shorter Catechism explains man's purpose: "Man's chief end is to glorify God and to enjoy him forever." How does the prayer that Paul offers for the Philippians in 1:9–11 reflect both aspects of this "chief end"?

15. The doctrine of the *providence* of God teaches us not only that God knows everything that will happen but that he actually orders and ordains everything that does happen, for his glory and his people's eternal good. How does Paul's attitude about his imprisonment and his ministry rivals demonstrate the deep trust he has in the providence of God?

APPLYING THE TEXT

16. What can you learn from Paul's prayer (1:9–11) about how to pray for yourself and for other believers?

17. How does the way that Paul reacts to his imprisonment (1:12–14) tell you that you should respond to suffering, trials, and hardship in your own life? Does anything in this passage especially convict you?

18. Does your need for recognition sometimes hold you back from experiencing genuine joy in what God is doing around you? What should your response be when God uses others for his purposes? Consider how you may need to change in these areas.

PRAYER PROMPT

As you close your study of this passage, ask God to help you, by his Spirit, to enlarge your heart and mind and give you a heavenly and eternal perspective. Ask him to increase your knowledge, love, and discernment. Implore him for a heart that is able to rejoice when the gospel advances—even when this requires you to suffer and when your contributions are not recognized. Pray to be able to rejoice, like Paul, in any circumstance in which Christ is glorified.

Finding Freedom, pgs. 66–67
Do you need to be set free from the feverish quest to be best, to be first, or to achieve and gain recognition? Are you frustrated and bitter when it doesn't happen . . . ? Only one person can set your heart free from the heavy burden of your own reputation, free to sing in a cell . . . , to rejoice in the success of your rivals, and to put your life on the line for a cause bigger than yourself. . . . That person is the Lord Jesus whom Paul served.

LESSON 3

A TOUGH CHOICE—BUT ONE SUPREME GOAL

Philippians 1:18–26

THE BIG PICTURE

Paul has been rejoicing over the fact that the gospel has grown through his imprisonment and his rivals' preaching; and now, in the passage we will study for this lesson, he moves on to wrestling with a tough choice: Which is better—life . . . or death? As he sits imprisoned and uncertain of his immediate fate, which of these outcomes ought Paul to desire and to pray that Jesus will grant him? While he wrestles through this quandary, we clearly see the call he has received for his life and the confidence he has regarding death.

Paul believes that he will be delivered, and he knows that ultimately Christ will be honored whether he lives or dies (1:18–20). For Paul, the reality is simple: if he goes on living, he will glorify, praise, and proclaim Jesus Christ; if he dies, he will enter the presence of his beloved Savior (1:21). Still, the choice is difficult! While he longs to depart and be with Jesus, he values the labor of love he has been performing on behalf of Christ and the people of God (1:22–24). His love for the saints God has entrusted to him, and his desire to nurture them in the faith, cause Paul to conclude that he would best glorify God by continuing to live and preach and by pursuing their "progress and joy in the faith" (1:25–26).

This passage shows us a soul that is completely at peace—the apostle Paul is content to labor on for the sake of the gospel but also ready to die at any moment and meet the Savior he proclaims. What a model he is for Christians today! He is our guide as we too consider the calling we have received for our lives and the benefits that will be ours through death.

Read Philippians 1:18–26.

GETTING STARTED

1. What kinds of difficulties might lead someone to long to be released from their suffering through death? How does Jesus Christ provide hope for suffering people who are considering life and death?

2. Why are some people (and even Christians) terrified of death? When Christians cling desperately to life, what truths—about both life and death—are they likely forgetting?

Alternative Routes, pgs. 70–71

[Paul's] certainty of reaching his destination casts a distinctive light on the alternative routes that lie before him—ongoing life or impending death. The advantages of each option compound his dilemma in choosing which of them he should request from his sovereign Savior. In the end, though, Paul's supreme goal so transforms his deepest desire that it "tips the scale" of his own preference in the direction of ongoing life for the sake of promoting others' progress and joy in trusting Jesus.

OBSERVING THE TEXT

3. What is the foundation of the confidence, joy, and hope that Paul displays throughout this passage?

4. What genuine struggle does Paul articulate while he is considering both life and death (1:22–24)? What makes choosing between the two genuinely difficult for him—and what factors does he consider about each?

5. Paul models how to straightforwardly consider death and mortality throughout this passage. How does his use of language contrast with that of many people who are approaching the topic of death?

UNDERSTANDING THE TEXT

6. As Paul, from the midst of his imprisonment, considers what lies ahead of him, what is his cause for confidence? Since he says that he knows he will be delivered through others' prayers but is unsure whether he will be released from prison or executed (see also 2:17), what type of "deliverance" must he have in mind? What is his "eager expectation and hope," and his chief motivation, regardless of what happens to him (1:18–20)?

7. Philippians 1:21 beautifully and succinctly captures the right way for a person who belongs to Jesus Christ to view both life and death. What does Paul mean when he says that to live "is Christ"? What does a Christian gain through death?

8. What benefits does Paul identify of both the potential outcomes before him (1:22–23)? Which outcome would benefit others, as well as Paul himself, and how?

9. How does Paul weigh the Christ-honoring good that will result, no matter what happens to him (1:23–24)? What seems to tip the scales for him (v. 24)?

10. What fruit does Paul hope will result in the lives of the Philippian believers if he continues to live, minister, and preach (1:25–26)?

11. What fundamental truths about our *calling* in life does this passage teach us? What parts of it demonstrate the *confidence* that those of us who belong to Jesus Christ by faith are to have in the face of death?

BIBLE CONNECTIONS

12. Read 2 Corinthians 5:8. What agreement do you see between the affirmation that Paul makes in that verse and the sentiment he expresses in our passage for this lesson? What reaction should Christians have to this description of what their state will be after death, and why?

Torn between Two Advantages, pg. 77
For Paul, . . . both ongoing life in this world and sudden death have almost irresistible advantages, though they are not advantages that would occur either to those who are suicidal or to those who cling desperately to this life.

13. In John 16:5–7, Jesus himself weighs the benefits of remaining with his disciples against those of returning to his Father in heaven. What benefit that will result from his departure does he reveal to his disciples—and how should this encourage those of us who follow him today?

THEOLOGY CONNECTIONS

14. Paul desires to depart and be "with Christ" (1:23). The Westminster Confession of Faith explains that "the bodies of men, after death, return to dust and see corruption; but their souls . . . immediately return to God who gave them. The souls of the righteous, being then made perfect in holiness, are received into the highest heavens, where they behold the face of God . . . waiting for the full redemption of their bodies" (32.1). What additional light does this shed on Paul's perspective that death will be "far better" for him than life (1:23)?

15. This passage indicates that believers are present with Christ immediately after they die, and, as the Westminster Confession of Faith quotation above reminds us, their souls will be united to glorified resurrection bodies on the last day. How can these truths inform our grief and sorrow when believing loved ones die?

APPLYING THE TEXT

16. Paul's hope is that Christ would be "honored" in his "body"—whether in life or in death (1:20). When we have the same hope, how will it shape our prayers—for both ourselves and others—in times when we are sick, suffering, or even approaching death?

17. What do you find convicting about Paul's concern for both the proclamation of the gospel and the spiritual health of the Philippian believers? To what degree does your own calling incorporate building up the believers in your midst—and does that need to change, in any way, in light of this passage?

18. What comfort does this passage offer to those who are close to death? What confidence does it give you as you consider your own mortality?

Supremely Satisfying, pg. 74
What is your supreme goal in life, your "eager expectation and hope" (Phil. 1:20)? Paul expressed his supreme goal—to promote Jesus' glory, whatever the cost or benefit to Paul himself—in order to whet the Philippians' and our appetites for the same heart-satisfying aim.

PRAYER PROMPT

As you close your study of this beautiful passage of Scripture, ask God to grant you the perspective the apostle Paul had on both life and death. Ask him for the Spirit's help so that you can view your life as "Christ"—as being lived for his glory, praise, and proclamation. Pray that he would give you the confidence, even as you consider death, that comes from knowing that death in Christ means being present with him—both immediately and for eternity to come.

LESSON 4

SOLIDARITY IN SUFFERING

Philippians 1:27–30

THE BIG PICTURE

In this lesson, you will focus on just four short verses—which are rich and packed full of meaning and application for God's faithful disciples in every age. Paul wrote them to believers who faced significant opposition, hardship, and social pressure as they lived for Jesus in Philippi—a Roman colony in Macedonia. Surrounded by idol-worshipers who lived sinful and selfish lives, the Philippian Christians were called to willingly share in the suffering of their Savior and of his servant Paul as well.

Paul begins these verses by focusing the Philippians on their own conduct and the relationships they have with one another in the church; they are to live lives that are "worthy" of the gospel and commit to being united with one another "for the faith of the gospel" (1:27). They are not to let their opponents frighten them. Rather, their steadfast holiness and courage will bear witness to their true salvation—as well as to the eventual judgment of those who oppose Jesus and the church (1:28). Paul concludes this brief passage by reminding his audience of the proper perspective for Christians to take: that when they endure abuse and persecution because they "believe" in Jesus Christ, they have been granted the great privilege of sharing in his suffering (1:29). He reminds them, as well, that they share not only in the suffering of Christ but also in the sufferings of his servants—such as Paul, who endured conflict in Philippi when he first preached the gospel there (1:30).

Paul's call to the Philippians resonates with all Christians who face hostility, verbal abuse, or negative pressure because of their devotion to Jesus and his gospel. We are called to walk in a way that is worthy of the gospel, and to maintain loving unity with our brothers and sisters in Christ, as we learn to share in the far greater suffering he endured for our sake.

Read Philippians 1:27–30.

GETTING STARTED

1. Think of a time when you saw a hardship or difficulty put pressure on a team, company, group, or family. What happened to the relationships between the people in that group?

2. What lies are Christians tempted to believe (about God, themselves, and so on) when they are faced with suffering or hardship while faithfully serving Jesus?

Courage Comes through Grace, pg. 88

We must show courage that does not blink when opponents confront us, along with concern for fellow Christians with whom we stand, shoulder to shoulder. This new way of responding to the pressures of a society that has no sympathy for our faith is grounded in a deepening appreciation for the privileged status that Christ has conferred upon us by his grace.

OBSERVING THE TEXT

3. What encouraging words and truths does Paul offer to the suffering believers in Philippi throughout this passage?

4. What implicit warnings do Paul's instructions in 1:27–28 contain regarding the Philippians' potential responses to persecution and hardship?

5. What makes Paul's personal love and concern for the Philippian Christians evident in this passage (see 1:27, 30)?

UNDERSTANDING THE TEXT

6. Why does Paul remind these Philippian believers, who are facing persecution, to "let [their] manner of life be worthy of the gospel" (1:27)? What temptations might they experience to respond to opposition in sinful ways?

7. Why do you think Paul sees a need to call the Philippian church to strive for unity during this time of persecution together (1:27)? What might tempt them to cease striving "side by side" for the gospel as they suffer?

8. Why would believers living in first-century Philippi (a Roman colony that was full of retired soldiers and idol-worshippers) have been tempted to live in fear, as the first half of verse 28 warns against? Why is it important for believers not to be frightened by those who oppose them? How can they resist their fear?

9. Why does it serve as a sign of God's salvation when his people respond to persecution in a fearless, holy, and unified way (1:28)? How does their faithfulness hint at the "destruction" that is to come for all those who oppose Jesus and his gospel?

10. What glorious truth does Paul offer to the Philippians about their suffering and the way it relates to the suffering of Jesus Christ (1:29)? What makes this an encouraging truth for those who endure persecution?

11. How does Paul connect the sufferings of the Philippians to the suffer-ings he himself has undergone for the gospel—and how would this be encouraging for a church such as the one in Philippi (1:30)?

BIBLE CONNECTIONS

12. Acts 16:16–24 describes some of the "conflict" the Philippian believers had witnessed Paul facing in their city. Read those verses now. Why do you think Paul found it important to remind the Philippian believers of the conflict and suffering he had faced for the sake of the gospel (1:30)?

13. Read 1 Peter 3:13–15. How does Peter address the potential "fear" of his audience? What commands does Peter give in these verses? What similarities do you see between his teaching and Paul's teaching?

Persecution in Philippi, pg. 87
We do not know the exact form of the Philippians' suffering for the sake of Christ, but Paul compares their sufferings with his own: both those that they saw him experience in Philippi and those that he now endures in Rome, as they have heard. So it is safe to say that their suffering had already been more severe than the mild ways in which Christians are currently marginalized in the West, and was more akin to the oppression endured today by believers in the developing world.

THEOLOGY CONNECTIONS

14. Paul calls the Philippians to walk in a way that is "worthy" of the gospel (1:27). Why is this *always* an important reminder for believers in Jesus, no matter where they are in their spiritual journey? As you write your response, consider answer 78 of the Westminster Larger Catechism: "The imperfection of sanctification in believers arises from the remnants of sin abiding in every part of them, and the perpetual lustings of the flesh against the spirit; whereby they are often foiled with temptations, and fall into many sins."

15. Paul tells the suffering Christians in Philippi that it has been "granted" to them to suffer for the sake of Christ (1:29). Why do you think that suffering for Christ can be considered a gracious gift from God? See Acts 5:41 for the way the apostles understood the suffering they experienced for the gospel.

A Call to the Citizens of Heaven, pg. 99
Citizens of heaven, behave in ways befitting the character of your King, who rules now and will return in glory. By his transforming grace, show courageous humility, bold gentleness, and selfless solidarity, calmly enduring all that this decomposing culture can throw at you. All the while, invite the very people who would intimidate you to share in the gifts of the King's grace, to join you in believing in him and in suffering for his sake.

APPLYING THE TEXT

16. What aspects of facing hardship or opposition to your faith tempt you to stop walking in a way that is worthy of the gospel? What actions, words, or thoughts do you need to repent of related to this? What can you do today to renew your commitment to holiness and obedience?

17. How can you pursue gospel unity, and strive "side by side" for the faith of the gospel (1:27), with fellow Christians? What obstacles have you experienced getting in the way of this gospel unity—particularly when you and fellow Christians are undergoing times of pressure and tension?

18. How can Philippians 1:29 shape your understanding of any suffering or hardship that afflicts you *as a result* of your devotion to Jesus Christ or your proclamation of his gospel?

PRAYER PROMPT

As you close this lesson, begin praying by first asking God to help you to remember brothers and sisters who belong to Christ and are suffering violent and fierce persecution for their belief in the gospel. Pray for members of the body of Christ who are facing the threat of death, imprisonment, and other forms of violent opposition to their faith. Then pray for your local community of believers—ask God to help those in your church to walk in a way that is worthy of the gospel and to strive for loving unity in Christ. Pray for courage so that you can stand for Jesus—even when that comes at great cost.

LESSON 5

HEARTS TURNED INSIDE OUT

Philippians 2:1–4

THE BIG PICTURE

Paul has been guiding the Philippians' hearts by emphasizing the importance of proclaiming the gospel—no matter the circumstance, situation, or suffering they are facing. He calls them to rejoice, as he himself does, when the gospel of Jesus Christ advances—as it has even in the midst of his imprisonment! Now, at the start of chapter 2, Paul directs the Philippians' eyes toward one another and calls them to the unnatural, Spirit-empowered task of living in unity and looking to the interests of others in the body before their own.

The apostle assumes that the genuine work of the Spirit has been guiding the Philippian church and the individual Christians there; they have experienced "encouragement in Christ," "comfort from love," "participation in the Spirit," and "affection and sympathy" from God, one another, and Paul himself (2:1). On the basis of these gifts they have received from God, Paul calls the church to make his "joy" complete by being united together in Christ (2:2). As they pursue this unity, he calls them to reject "selfish ambition" and "conceit" and to instead embrace a kind of "humility" that enables them to count other believers as being more "significant" than themselves (2:3). The Spirit-led Christian should look not only to his or her own interests but also to the interests of others who are in the body of Christ (2:4).

As we will find out later in the letter, there is some discord in the church at Philippi. Since he has heard about this, Paul now addresses their lack of unity as well as their self-interest and pride. In order for the church to be truly gospel centered, the hearts of God's people must more and more resemble the selfless, giving, and humble heart of our Savior King, who looked eternally and gloriously toward the interests of others in order to accomplish their salvation at the cross.

Read Philippians 2:1–4.

GETTING STARTED

1. What would you identify as some of the biggest threats to the church in your culture today? Why do these threats seem particularly dangerous?

2. Describe a time when you prioritized yourself and your own needs, comforts, or interests. Why is it so difficult for us to consider the perspectives, interests, and well-being of others?

A Real Threat, pg. 102

[Paul] would hardly waste his breath forbidding "rivalry or conceit" (Phil. 2:3) and urging each to care for others' interests unless some, at least, were focusing on their own concerns and agendas, neglecting those in need, and jeopardizing the congregation's unity. Paul would not amass reasons for staying unified in heart and mind . . . unless the oneness of conviction and affection in this church at Philippi, whom he loved so dearly, faced a real threat.

OBSERVING THE TEXT

3. What are the various phrases Paul uses in 2:2 to describe the unity to which he calls the Philippian church? What particular aspect of unity in the church does each phrase identify?

4. Based on the commands Paul issues in this passage, what can we assume was going on in the church at Philippi? What might this have looked like?

5. The commands in this passage go against our natural tendencies. What enables us to obey them?

UNDERSTANDING THE TEXT

6. How do the commands that Paul issues in Philippians 2:2–4 relate to the phrases he uses in verse 1? What functions as evidence of the Spirit's genuine work in the life of a church, and why?

7. Why do you think Paul mentions his own "joy" in verse 2? What effect does this have on the commands and appeals he then issues?

8. What kinds of motivation does Paul forbid his hearers from having in 2:3? What makes "selfish ambition" and "conceit" into forces that are incredibly dangerous to the church if they take root in the hearts of believers?

9. What is the root and foundation of Paul's commands (2:3)? What does it mean to count others as being more "significant" than ourselves? Practically speaking, what would this look like in the church—both then and now?

10. What does it take for us to consider the "interests of others" (2:4)? What sorts of disciplines, practices, and behaviors can we develop in order to better care for others in our Christian communities?

11. The work that Jesus Christ performed on the cross serves as our ultimate example for the behaviors and attitudes that Paul calls the Philippians to adopt in this passage. Why is it dangerous to seek to obey these verses without first turning to our Savior and his cross?

BIBLE CONNECTIONS

12. Read 1 Corinthians 1:10–17. What echoes do you see between the calls to unity that Paul issues to the church in Corinth and the call that he gives in Philippians 2:1–2? What did the divisions and disunity in the church in Corinth seem to be based on?

13. Read Mark 12:28–34, in which Jesus teaches about the two greatest commandments. How does Paul's teaching in Philippians 2:1–4 serve to apply the teaching of the second greatest commandment?

The Strong Bond of Affection, pg. 107

It's as if Paul is saying, "It is not enough to agree with each other theologically: God actually calls you to *care for* each other deeply, in a love that binds your souls together so strongly that differences of perspective cannot pull you apart." This strong bond of affection, grounded in the truth of the gospel, stabilizes believers' relationships with each other so that they can address their differences—whether doctrinal or interpersonal—in patience, humility, and love.

THEOLOGY CONNECTIONS

14. According to question and answer 167 of the Westminster Larger Catechism, part of the way we "improve" on our baptism is by seeking "to walk in brotherly love, as being baptized by the same Spirit into one body." According to the catechism, what does our baptism do to lead us to live in loving unity with others in the church?

15. The Puritan preacher Jonathan Edwards once remarked, "We must view humility as one of the most essential things that characterizes true Christianity."[1] Do you agree with this? If so, why?

APPLYING THE TEXT

16. Do you tend more to have disagreement and discord with other believers or to pursue gospel-powered unity with them in Jesus Christ? How would you rate your discernment about knowing when to fight for truth? Have you been able to lovingly disagree with others in the church without sacrificing a spirit of unity? In what ways may you need to change or grow regarding this?

1. Jonathan Edwards, *Faith beyond Feelings: Discerning the Heart of True Spirituality*, ed. James M. Houston (Colorado Springs: David C. Cook, 2004), 153.

17. What tempts you to count yourself as being more "significant" than others (Phil. 2:3)? Why is it so difficult to do the opposite—and what practical steps might you take, through prayer and through your efforts, to become more obedient in this area?

18. As you seek to obey the commands of Philippians 2:1–4, what motivation and guidance do you need to take from Jesus's sacrifice and example?

A New Desire, pg. 111

The others-embracing, others-serving mind-set of Christ is so unnatural to our self-preserving instincts. Yet when God's grace grasps us deeply, it begins to develop into our deepest, strongest desire. We begin to care for all our brothers and sisters in Christ with the same passionate intensity that we so automatically and easily lavish on our own comforts and concerns.

PRAYER PROMPT

As you close your study of this brief and yet powerful passage, spend some time asking God to change your heart more and more so that it reflects this "others-embracing, others-serving" mindset.[2] Confess your failures and your weakness to God, with the knowledge that he understands your selfish instincts and desires! Pray that he would help you to follow in the path of your Savior by seeking unity with other believers and pursuing their well-being—even more than you pursue your own.

---

2. See Dennis E. Johnson, *Philippians*, Reformed Expository Commentary (Phillipsburg, NJ: P&R Publishing, 2013), 111.

LESSON 6

STOOPING KING; EXALTED SON

Philippians 2:5–11

THE BIG PICTURE

We saw in the previous lesson that Paul has been calling the Philippian believers to pursue unity with one another in the church, as well as to hold attitudes of humility, selflessness, and deference toward each other. Now he comes to the glorious gospel foundation of the call he has been issuing: the humiliation and exaltation of the Lord Jesus Christ. Through his humble descent to humanity—and ultimately through his death on the cross—Christ not only accomplishes salvation but also serves as the great example of humility that his people should follow. In Christ's ascent to glory, our God reminds us of his eternal reign—and of the path from humiliation to exaltation that we follow by putting our faith in the Savior who has walked it as well.

Paul links this passage to the preceding four verses of the chapter by giving an additional command: "Have this mind among yourselves, which is yours in Christ Jesus" (2:5). Then he traces the humbling descent of Jesus, who laid aside the rights and privileges that were his as God, descended to earth as an actual human being, and even humbled himself to the level of undergoing the excruciating pain and utter humiliation of his sacrificial death on the cross (2:6–8). Precisely *because* he carried out our salvation by humbling himself according to the will of God, the Father has now exalted Jesus above every name in the universe (2:9). In fact, there will come a day when every voice in the entire cosmos will acknowledge his eternal reign and glory (2:10–11).

Paul's description of the earthly humiliation and eternal glorification of Jesus gives us not only a reason to hope for salvation from our sin but also an example for us to follow as we live for Jesus. Followers of Jesus are to have the "mind" of Christ (v. 5)—to humble themselves as they serve one another. Yet even in their humility, they hope for ultimate vindication, glorification, and eternal joy in the presence of their exalted Savior and Lord.

Read Philippians 2:5–11.

GETTING STARTED

1. Describe a time when you were humbled in some way. What effect did this have on your heart and mind? Has being humbled enabled you, or someone else you know, to grow? How?

2. Why do you think some people in the church emphasize the role Jesus has as our *Savior* but not as our *example*? What dangers might they be trying to avoid? Why is it important for us to emphasize both of these roles?

A Pinnacle of Theological Truth, pg. 119
This passage is . . . a majestic mountain peak, towering over the surrounding countryside. It is a pinnacle of theological truth, piercing the heavens and probing the mystery of the incarnation. Its dramatic movement traces the inverted arc of Christ's redemptive mission from divine glory down into humiliation and death, and then up again to heaven's heights in resurrection splendor.

OBSERVING THE TEXT

3. How does Paul make it clear in Philippians 2:5 that his teaching about Jesus will directly impact the lives and attitudes of the Philippian believers?

4. How would you describe the overall *shape* of this passage—particularly throughout 2:6–11? Why is this shape an important part of helping us to understand both the life and the work of Jesus as well as the lives we live as Christians?

5. What theological doctrines does this brief passage explain or apply? What makes these doctrines fundamental to the Christian faith?

UNDERSTANDING THE TEXT

6. What command do we see in Philippians 2:5? What does this verse tell us is true of Christians who seek to obey this command?

7. What does 2:6 teach us about Jesus's attitude about power and service? How should his attitude shape our own view of our rights and privileges?

8. In the incarnation, Jesus became fully human while remaining fully God. So in what sense did Jesus "empty" himself when he took on human flesh and came to earth (2:7)?

9. Undergoing the humiliation of the cross was a matter of obedience for Jesus (2:8). Who was he obeying? Why?

10. What did God do in response to Jesus's obedient humiliation (2:9)? What is Jesus's status now, in comparison to the status he held both on earth and prior to his incarnation?

More Than an Example, pg. 130

[Christ's] self-humbling defines the humility of mind that will enable the Philippians to count others more significant than themselves. . . . His obedience sets the pace for their ongoing obedience to the will of God. . . . But his humility and obedience to death did more than set a noble example. As the Lamb of God, by his blood he "ransomed people for God from every tribe and language and people and nation" (Rev. 5:9).

11. Jesus is exalted at the right hand of God the Father, even though he is not acknowledged as King and Savior by all on earth. What do we learn in Philippians 2:10–11 about Jesus's final and ultimate exaltation? What will happen one day? What makes this good news for some and bad news for others?

BIBLE CONNECTIONS

12. Perhaps the most debated aspect of this passage is Paul's use in 2:7 of the Greek word *kenoo*, which carries the connotation of "emptying" or "setting aside." While it is important for us to understand that Jesus set aside the *rights and privileges* of his deity when he became incarnate, we must not misunderstand this to mean that he set aside his deity *itself*. When Jesus took on flesh and became completely human, he never ceased being completely God. Read the interaction that Jesus has with the Jewish leaders in John 8:48–59. In what way does he clearly bear witness to his full divinity—and what is the Jews' reaction?

13. Read Isaiah 53:1–6. What stands out to you as you read this prophetic description of the Messiah's humiliation? How can Isaiah's words help you to better understand Philippians 2:5–8?

THEOLOGY CONNECTIONS

14. Answer 27 of the Westminster Shorter Catechism explains that "Christ's humiliation consisted in his being born, and that in a low condition, made under the law, undergoing the miseries of this life, the wrath of God, and the cursed death of the cross; in being buried, and continuing under the power of death for a time." What aspects of Christ's "humiliation" do you or other believers sometimes underemphasize? How can his humiliation help to shape your understanding of your own discipleship and walk with Christ?

15. Question 50 of the Heidelberg Catechism teaches that "Christ ascended into heaven for this end, that he might there appear as head of his church, by whom the Father governs all things." What does this teach us about Christ's reign as it currently manifests itself? What will change about how visible that reign is, and when will this happen, according to Philippians 2:10–11?

The Highest Splendor Imaginable, pg. 141
Our text . . . celebrates One whom God the Father has appropriately exalted above all, the Son who is eternally the Father's equal and who thus deserves total worship from every creature everywhere. The three persons of the triune God . . . delight to magnify one another. They are right to do so, for each deserves the highest splendor imaginable—even beyond the bounds of our finite imaginations!

APPLYING THE TEXT

16. How do you think your relationships would change if you more fully embraced the humble "mind" evidenced by Jesus Christ your Savior? Consider specific relationships within your family, church, and group of friends.

17. What do the descent and ascent of Jesus teach you about suffering and hardship in the Christian life? What is your hope regarding eternity?

18. Why should the fact that Jesus will ultimately be glorified throughout all creation motivate us to take part in evangelism—the verbal witness of the message of the gospel? How should the picture that we see in Philippians 2:10–11 shape our perspective on earthly authorities, trials, and even suffering?

PRAYER PROMPT

As you close your study of this beautifully rich passage, praise God the Father for the saving work he performed through God the Son and applied to your heart through the power of God the Holy Spirit. Praise God that he, the eternal triune ruler, delights to magnify himself by saving sinners like you! Then ask him to give you more and more of the mind of Christ. Ask him to enable you to follow the example of humility that he displayed on the cross as you also hope to be glorified eternally in the presence of your risen and exalted Savior.

LESSON 7

SHINING STARS

Philippians 2:12–18

THE BIG PICTURE

After calling the Philippian believers to pursue unity and selfless love, and reminding them of the divine example of their Savior's humiliation and exaltation, Paul now moves on to give more practical instructions to these believers who are living out their faith in a context of social marginalization and persecution. He tells them to humbly work out their salvation with joyful contentment, patience, and sacrifice, since this will glorify God and aid their gospel witness.

Paul calls the Philippians to "work out" their salvation in humility, with the knowledge that God himself is the one working in them for his glorious pleasure (2:12–13). Here is a command for believers to put effort into pursuing obedience and sanctification through the power of God's Spirit. The working out of our own salvation must happen in conjunction with patience and contentment, and this will not only preserve unity in the church but also enable us to be a shining witness to a watching and unbelieving world (2:14–15). As Paul issues these commands, he speaks again of the joyful suffering he himself has undergone on behalf of these believers; he is willing to be poured out like a "drink offering" for the sake of their faith and growth in Christ (2:16–18). The apostle invites the believers to rejoice with him over both his calling and theirs—a calling that may indeed require them to follow in the same path of suffering that he has walked for the gospel.

We should be encouraged by the example of these first-century believers, who faced, as we do, disunity from within the church as well as societal pressures from without. We are called, as they were, to pursue unity through the gospel, contentment and patience, and a willingness to follow in the shadow of the cross as we proclaim the Savior.

Read Philippians 2:12–18.

GETTING STARTED

1. Consider your own walk with God: Are you more likely to fall into a "works righteousness" mentality (in which you to seek to earn God's favor) or a "presumption upon grace" mentality (in which you feel little need to discipline yourself to grow in holiness)? Explain your answer.

2. How do bad attitudes, disunity, and grumbling in the church affect Christians' witness to the watching world? What results have you seen when Christians have had such a "witness"?

Characteristics of Heavenly Citizens, pg. 154
[Paul] is continuing the motif of behavior befitting citizens of heaven, strangers sojourning briefly on the earth as we journey toward the celestial city that is our true home. He focuses on two characteristics of our heavenly citizenship, which make us stand out from the culture around us: (1) sober and hopeful obedience, and (2) patient and selfless contentment.

OBSERVING THE TEXT

3. How does the command in 2:12 for us to "work out [our] own salvation" fit together with the truth in 2:13 that God is the one working in us? What tensions exist between these verses?

4. In this passage, Paul calls the church to consider how it appears to the watching world. What images does he use to describe its witness?

5. What do you notice about Paul's description of his ministry to the Philippians and the love he has for them (2:16–18)? What do these verses reveal about his heart and the sacrificial commitment he has made for their sake?

UNDERSTANDING THE TEXT

6. What does Paul say should characterize the Philippian believers' pursuit of obedience and the growth of their holiness (2:12)? What attitude and mindset do the words "fear" and "trembling" imply—and how should they shape the way we approach living in Christ and growing through our sanctification?

7. What truths does Paul teach in 2:13 about our walk with God and our growth in Christ? How ought these truths to impact our efforts to obey God and practice spiritual discipline?

8. What warning does Paul give in 2:14—and what might tempt believers, within any church context, to engage in those sinful behaviors?

9. How does Paul direct the Philippians to consider their external witness as well as their internal unity (2:15)? What does this verse teach us about the role our personal holiness, peace, and contentment play in our evangelism and gospel proclamation?

Christ Does It All, pg. 158

In rescuing us from sin's guilt and punishment, Christ does it all *apart from* us: he obeys in our place, suffers in our place, rises to victorious life in our place, and even gives us faith by his Spirit. . . . On the other hand, in rescuing us from sin's controlling power, Christ still does it all, but he does it *through* us: his Spirit enlivens, enlists, and enables us as allies.

10. Paul again makes personal comments in 2:16–17, which reveal the heart he has for the Philippian church. What does verse 16 say would assure him that he had not labored "in vain" over them? How does the sacrificial imagery that he uses in verse 17 help you to understand Paul's own sense of the apostolic calling he has received for the sake of these first-century believers and churches?

11. What attitude does Paul say the Philippians should have regarding his suffering and sacrifice for the sake of the gospel (2:18)? What gentle encouragement does this verse also offer them about the way they should understand the prospect of their own suffering and hardship for the sake of the advancement of the gospel?

BIBLE CONNECTIONS

12. Read 2 Peter 1:3–7, in which the apostle Peter also calls Christians to pursue holiness and obedience. What makes it impossible to mistake Peter's call, about expending work and "effort" (v. 5), for works righteousness?

13. Read Numbers 28:7–8. Based on this Old Testament context, what might Paul be implying in Philippians 2:17–18 about the role that he, as well as the Philippians and other believers, play in the gospel? What does it tell us about the attitude he has as a servant of the gospel?

THEOLOGY CONNECTIONS

14. Answer 115 of the Heidelberg Catechism explains that the commandments of God are to be preached so that "we may constantly endeavor, and pray to God for the grace of the Holy Spirit, to be renewed more and more after the image of God, till after this life we arrive at the goal of perfection." What agreement do you see between this instruction and the apostle Paul's from Philippians 2:12?

15. Answer 35 of the Westminster Shorter Catechism defines *sanctification* as "the work of God's free grace, whereby we are renewed in the whole man after the image of God, and are enabled more and more to die unto sin, and live unto righteousness." How does this definition help to explain Paul's assertion to the Philippians that God "works in" them (2:13)?

APPLYING THE TEXT

16. Consider your efforts to obey God, practice the spiritual disciplines, and grow in Christ. In which areas do you need more encouragement? Who could you ask to hold you accountable to this good work?

17. What situations (or people) tempt you to grumble and complain? How can this passage serve as a call for you to repent from doing this and grow in the areas of joy and contentment?

18. What can you do to witness more intentionally to those around you who do not know Christ? What aspects of your life, speech, and personal interactions could God use as a light for those who need to know and believe the gospel?

A Surprising Route to Joy, pg. 165
[Paul's] purpose is not to sound a sour note amid his encouragement. Rather, he is leading his dear friends back to his recurring theme of joy by a surprising route. Even Paul's death, whether it occurs sooner or later, will be symptomatic of the suffering entailed in believers' calling to shine like stars in a dark universe, to live for Jesus amid a crooked generation.

PRAYER PROMPT

By God's grace, you are called, as the Philippian believers were, to "work out your own salvation" humbly and intentionally while at the same time trusting in the divine and sovereign work God is performing in your heart and soul. Today, pray that God would continue the good work he is doing in you as well as in your church. Ask him to help your holiness, joy, contentment, and patience to grow—for the sake of not only the internal unity of your church but also your gospel witness to an external, watching world. Ask him to make you willing to endure hardship, discomfort, and even suffering as you follow Jesus and make him known.

LESSON 8

LIVING REPLICAS

Philippians 2:19–30

THE BIG PICTURE

The passage we will study during this lesson will put before you two "living replicas of the servant of the Lord"—men whom the apostle Paul holds out to the Philippians as faithful servants of Jesus Christ and friends to him in his gospel ministry.[1] In Timothy and Epaphroditus, we see an exemplary faithfulness that all Christians should seek to imitate as they support the work of the gospel that takes place throughout the world.

Paul describes Timothy, a young pastor who is with him at the time of this letter's composition, as one who seeks the "interests" of Jesus Christ in both his love for God's people and his support of Paul and his gospel ministry (2:19–24). While Paul cannot bear to release him yet, he tells the Philippians that he longs to send Timothy to them soon, so that they will be encouraged by his presence (vv. 19, 23). This young man, who has been like a "son" to Paul (v. 22), serves as a model for how God's people, in every age, are to support gospel work and gospel workers.

As we will see in 4:18, Epaphroditus had brought Paul a donation from the Philippians. Many scholars infer that he will go on to carry this letter from Paul to the Philippian church. Paul knows that the Philippians will be greatly encouraged and cheered when Epaphroditus arrives (2:25–30).

---

1. See chapter 11 in Dennis E. Johnson, *Philippians*, Reformed Expository Commentary (Phillipsburg, NJ: P&R Publishing, 2013).

He had been very ill—in fact, near death—much to the concern of all (v. 27). Now that he has recovered, Paul is sending him to these Christians and giving them a command to "honor" men such as him (v. 29)—men who have sacrificed much for the growth of the gospel.

Read Philippians 2:19–30.

GETTING STARTED

1. Who are some faithful Christians who have been role models to you? Why have you found their examples to be so compelling?

2. Think of successful leaders you know. What kind of helpers and support system do they have? Why is it important to acknowledge and remember the behind-the-scenes workers and helpers who are involved in any great work or cause?

The Heartbeat of Christ, pg. 169

Our text teaches . . . that God does embed into our experience living, breathing replicas of Jesus: men and women whose heart instincts are growing by grace so that we can sense the heartbeat of Christ in the way they treat others, react to adversity, and invest their energies. Watching them shows us what growing up to be like Jesus looks like in the nitty-gritty of everyday life.

OBSERVING THE TEXT

3. How would you describe the tone that characterizes Paul's description of Timothy and Epaphroditus in this passage? What does this tell you about the depth of the human relationships Paul enjoys in the midst of his gospel ministry?

4. What can you conclude about the work Timothy has done, and the relationship he has with Paul, from 2:19–24? What kind of young man does Timothy seem to be? What has made him such an encouragement to Paul?

5. What do you notice about the commands that Paul gives to the Philippians concerning Epaphroditus in 2:25–30? Why do you think they may need to hear these commands?

UNDERSTANDING THE TEXT

6. What phrases in Paul's description of Timothy speak to the intimate relationship and friendship the two of them share (2:19–24)? How does Paul view Timothy? What has Timothy offered Paul—and why does Paul value this so much?

7. Why does Paul want to send Timothy to the Philippians soon (2:19, 23)? What do you think Paul is hoping that Timothy will offer to the believers in Philippi—and what does he imply about the heart that Timothy has for them (2:20)?

8. As you look at the way Paul describes Epaphroditus's ministry and the encouragement he has offered, how does his description portray the way *suffering* has marked the life and gospel ministry of this man (2:25–30)? What metaphor does Paul use in verse 25 to describe their joint labor for the gospel—and what does this teach you about gospel ministry?

The Interests of Christ, pg. 175
Timothy will be an antidote to this spiritual toxemia [self-centeredness] infecting the Philippians. In his concern for them, they will see a man who seeks not his own interests but those of Jesus Christ. The interests of Jesus Christ are the welfare of his people.

9. What clues in 2:26 indicate that the Philippians have some relationship with, or knowledge of, Epaphroditus already? How did the Philippians' reaction to his sickness affect him emotionally?

10. Paul writes that Epaphroditus became sick as a direct result of his gospel ministry or missionary travels. How should believers receive and treat those who have suffered during their labors for the gospel (2:29–30)?

11. As you look over Philippians 2:19–30, how would you say Timothy and Epaphroditus imitated Jesus Christ in their lives and actions? What is Christlike about these two men?

BIBLE CONNECTIONS

12. Skim through 2 Samuel 23:8–39, and read at least some of the descriptions of the "mighty men" of King David who served and fought with him, especially during his wilderness years. In what way do Timothy and Epaphroditus serve as Paul's "mighty men"? What marked differences set their work apart from the military exploits performed by David's mighty men?

13. Read the greetings that Paul issues in Romans 16:3–16 to a number of men and women from the church in Rome. What do these personal greetings tell you about Paul's relationships with those in the early church? What does this imply about any attempts to engage in church life or gospel ministry as a "lone wolf"?

THEOLOGY CONNECTIONS

14. The Westminster Confession of Faith offers this beautiful description of the communion of saints: "Saints by profession are bound to maintain a holy fellowship and communion in the worship of God; and in performing such other spiritual services as tend to their mutual edification; as also in relieving each other in outward things, according to their several abilities, and necessities. Which communion, as God offers opportunity, is to be extended unto all those who, in every place, call upon the name of the Lord Jesus" (26.2). How does Paul demonstrate this "holy fellowship and communion" through his relationships with Timothy and Epaphroditus—and how do they demonstrate it through their own relationships with the Philippian church?

Servants of Jesus, pg. 185
Let Timothy show you what it looks like to push back against your own fears, and instead to have your heart opened to the cares and concerns of others. Let Epaphroditus show you the quiet courage that takes risks to health and safety, that puts one's own comforts and convenience in jeopardy, for the work of Christ, in service to the servants of Jesus.

15. While the Reformed Protestant tradition has rejected the veneration of saints, Paul does command us to "honor" servants of Christ who suffer and labor faithfully for the gospel (2:29–30). How can we sincerely and appropriately "honor" such men and women in a way that avoids veneration or idolatry?

APPLYING THE TEXT

16. Would other believers say of you what Paul said of Timothy—that you seek the "interests" of Jesus Christ and the "welfare" of others (2:20–21)? If you don't think so, why not? What can you do to better seek to imitate the godliness of Timothy?

17. What do Epaphroditus's sickness and suffering teach you about the path of cross-shaped discipleship? In what ways does your attitude need to change regarding the prospect of experiencing discomfort or trouble for the sake of the gospel?

18. How can you "honor" those who serve and proclaim Jesus even in the face of great suffering (2:29)? What can your church community do in order to better receive and honor faithful ministry workers?

PRAYER PROMPT

You have seen the joy Paul experiences because of Timothy—a selfless servant of the gospel. You have seen the way Paul honors Epaphroditus—a suffering servant of the gospel. Now, spend some time praying for God to give you the strength to imitate these servants of Christ—the same way they imitated their Savior as they served and proclaimed his gospel. Ask God to grant you the privilege of supporting gospel work and gospel workers; pray that he would help you to humbly honor those who give their lives in order to proclaim the Savior.

LESSON 9

TRADING MY RAGS FOR HIS ROBE

Philippians 3:1–11

THE BIG PICTURE

In this next section of his letter, Paul quickly turns from warning his readers to reflecting personally and worshipfully on the work the gospel has done in his own life. He says the Philippians must be on their guard against putting "confidence in the flesh" (v. 3). Paul writes as one who, because of the transforming work Jesus has done in his life, has learned to reject any confidence in his own fleshly qualifications and accomplishments and instead chosen to glorify only Christ, his Savior.

After encouraging the Philippians to "rejoice in the Lord" (3:1), Paul warns them about those who require circumcision and who treat it as an outward qualification of God's acceptance; he calls such people "dogs" who "mutilate the flesh" (3:2–3). Paul then turns to his own story and presents himself as a living example of what it means to reject boasting in oneself in favor of boasting in Jesus Christ alone (3:4–7). The apostle lists his human qualifications—his potential causes for confident boasting in his flesh—and describes his elite status as a Jew of Jews who was trained in the Hebrew Scriptures and immersed in a life of obedience to the Old Testament law. Now, though, he considers these fleshly qualifications to be "loss"—even "rubbish"—compared to the infinite worth of knowing Jesus Christ as his Savior (3:8).

Paul concludes this section with a description of his new gospel commitments, desires, and pursuits: namely, to follow Jesus by faith and to know him and the power of his resurrection more and more (3:9–11). The apostle calls the Philippians to reject legalism and human confidence and instead to rest in the riches of Christ's righteousness alone. Embracing the riches of Christ will enable them to joyfully reject self-righteousness, and all human qualifications, and see them as mere rags and rubbish.

Read Philippians 3:1–11.

GETTING STARTED

1. What outward qualifications are you tempted to rely on in order to be accepted by God—or by his people? In what ways would you say the church unwittingly supports this kind of thinking?

2. What hinders you from pressing on in humility to grow in your relationship with God? What would tempt you to feel that you have already "arrived"?

God's Free Grace, pg. 188
Paul rehearses his own experience as an example of God's free grace in Christ. He is safeguarding his friends in Philippi from a plausible spiritual poison spreading among the churches that he had planted among the Gentiles. . . . [False] teachers insisted that trust in Christ must be supplemented by circumcision and rigorous commandment-keeping, in order for Gentiles to find assurance of their standing among God's people and under God's favor.

OBSERVING THE TEXT

3. What can you conclude about the threat that Paul is concerned about on behalf of the believers in Philippi (3:2–3)? What kind of teaching or influence seems to be invading this church?

4. Why does Paul spend so much of this passage listing his earthly qualifications (3:4–6)? What point is he making—and what do the specific qualifications that he mentions imply about the teachers who are influencing the Philippian believers?

5. The final verses of this passage describe Paul's complete change of attitude, behavior, and motivation after he became a follower of Jesus (3:9–11). How do these verses serve as a kind of mission statement for the apostle?

An Energizing Force, pgs. 192–93
Paul could testify from his own experience that the path commended by the advocates of self-reliant law-keeping leads to a dead end, however promising it may appear at the trailhead. He has also found that resting in Christ and Christ's credentials actually energizes believers to pursue holiness and love with expectant eagerness.

UNDERSTANDING THE TEXT

6. Why do you think this passage begins with a command from Paul for the Philippians to "rejoice" in the Lord (3:1)? What occasion for rejoicing has he just mentioned, in 2:28? Based on what you have studied in this letter so far, what types of circumstances do you think might tempt them (as well as Paul) *not* to rejoice? What reasons has Paul already given for rejoicing, in 1:18–19, 25–26; 2:17–18?

7. How does Paul describe the opponents of the gospel of grace who are influencing the Philippians (3:2)? How would you characterize the tone he uses to do so—and what does this tell you about the nature of his warning?

8. What makes the qualifications that Paul lists in 3:4–6 so impressive from an earthly perspective? Why do you think he placed so much confidence in these human qualifications before his conversion?

9. How has Paul's perspective on his human qualifications and his causes for boasting changed since he came to faith in Jesus Christ (3:7–8)? What is now the source of his boasting, glory, and joy—and why?

10. What words and phrases within Philippians 3:9 provide a clear summary and defense of the doctrine of salvation by grace alone, through faith alone, and because of the righteousness of Christ alone?

11. What motivates Paul now that he is following Jesus Christ (3:10–11)? What is he hoping for, and what is he willing to endure as he follows his Savior?

Your Only Comfort, pg. 192

When you find yourself glorying in anything other than Christ Jesus, you need to return to the gracious gospel that drew you to your Savior at the beginning. You need to see that Christ, and Christ alone, deserves your full confidence, for Christ alone conveys "the righteousness from God" (Phil. 3:9) that silences Satan's charges and your own conscience's guilty discomfort.

BIBLE CONNECTIONS

12. Read Galatians 5:1–12. Note the intense and heated language Paul uses concerning the Judaizers and the members of the so-called "circumcision party" that is mentioned in Acts 11:2. Why does Paul see their particular brand of legalistic teaching as being such a threat to the gospel of grace? What similarities do you see between the tones he uses in this passage and in our passage from Philippians?

13. In 1 Corinthians 1:26–31, Paul describes the Corinthians in a way that sounds like the opposite of how he describes himself in Philippians 3:4–6. According to what he writes to them, what does the wisdom of the gospel do for those who have minimal worldly qualifications and causes for confidence?

THEOLOGY CONNECTIONS

14. According to the Westminster Confession of Faith, God justifies sinners by "accounting and accepting their persons as righteous, not for anything wrought in them, or done by them, but for Christ's sake alone" (11.1). What connection do you see between this statement and Paul's explanation of the foundation for his confidence? What makes justification a beautiful and freeing doctrine for sinners to believe?

15. The prophet Isaiah uses language similar to Paul's when he describes even our most righteous works as being filthy rags in comparison with the holiness and righteousness of God (Isa. 64:6). Why is believing in this truth important if we are to grasp our sinfulness and our need for God's grace? Once we have repented and put our faith in Christ alone, how is our obedience to Christ transformed, according to Ephesians 2:8–10? Are our righteous works able to please God our Father? Why, or why not?

APPLYING THE TEXT

16. What kinds of teaching today threaten to steer you toward trusting in your own righteousness, good works, or human qualifications rather than resting in the finished work of Jesus Christ alone? What could you do to lovingly warn others about these kinds of false teaching?

17. What do you need to remember about the way your own obedience and good deeds relate to the message of the gospel of Jesus Christ? Why is it essential for us to remember that we are saved by Christ's righteousness—not our own—and that our obedience is a response to his grace?

18. How can Paul's description of his goals and motivations, in Philippians 3:10–11, serve to shape the goals and motivations that you yourself have as a follower of Jesus? What practical changes would you say you need to make in your life so that you can better and more fully pursue these goals?

PRAYER PROMPT

The apostle Paul's conversion involved a complete recalibration of his sources of confidence and glory; what he once considered to be riches— his human qualifications—he now considered to be rags and rubbish as a result of coming to glory in the righteousness of Christ alone. Today, pray for this to be your story and testimony as well! Ask the Lord to do the work in your heart of destroying your confidence in your flesh, in your good works, and in any other qualifications that you are tempted to trust in rather than resting in the finished work he has performed on your behalf through Jesus Christ the Son. Pray for the humility you need in order to seek Jesus and for the willingness to suffer for his sake as you hope in the power of his resurrection.

LESSON 10

RESTLESS AND HOMELESS

Philippians 3:12–21

THE BIG PICTURE

In the previous lesson, we saw Paul repudiating his earthly and human qualifications and choosing instead to glory only in the righteousness of Jesus Christ his Savior. We saw that he counts the human things in which he used to have confidence as "rubbish" and lives now in the hope of Christ's resurrection—and that he calls the Philippians to adopt the same mindset.

Now Paul describes a sense of restlessness and holy discontent that he feels as he "press[es] on" to know Christ more and more (3:12). He makes it clear to the Philippian believers that he does not consider himself to be perfect but rather is living with a desire to continually grow in Christ as he keeps the final, heavenly prize always in view (3:13–14). Paul calls all "mature" believers to embrace this same mindset—to press onward toward Jesus and hold fast to the truth of the gospel (3:15–16).

As Paul describes his spiritual restlessness and desire for growth, he makes an important acknowledgment: true believers in Jesus are not at home in this world—they count heaven to be their true home and the place where their real citizenship lies (3:20–21). This perspective gives way to tearful sadness as Paul considers those who walk as "enemies" of Jesus Christ and his gospel (3:18–19). The Philippian believers, as they set their eyes on future glory, must continue following the example of Paul and of others who have modeled gospel faith in their lives and perspectives

(3:17). God's people in every age must also press on toward Christ as they are driven by the restlessness of those whose true citizenship is not of this earth.

Read Philippians 3:12–21.

GETTING STARTED

1. What have you seen people who are excellent in their professions do to train, improve, and educate themselves? What drives people to do this? Why do they seek to keep growing even though they are already successful?

2. What is the danger when a Christian starts to feel too "at home" in this world? Why does a sense of spiritual "homelessness" often function as a sign that we are following obediently after Jesus?

Drawn to the Feast, pg. 206

Paul's Philippian friends need to see in his own experience the truth that *everyone* who has tasted the firstfruits of God's reconciling and renewing grace will long to feast on the full banquet at their Father's table. So Paul continues his autobiography . . . , offering his current restless race as a "case study" in the response that grace evokes when it lays hold of a human heart.

OBSERVING THE TEXT

3. Read Philippians 3:9–11 in order to recall the context of this passage that follows. How do these verses set the stage for Paul's description of how he is restlessly "press[ing] on" in 3:12–13? Toward what goal and end is Paul pressing?

4. What makes it surprising that Paul, who was perhaps the greatest apostle, would embrace such an attitude of spiritual restlessness and a constant desire for growth?

5. What role does Christians' hope for the future play in Paul's teaching within the passage for this lesson? How does it shape our perspective on sin and suffering and give us a sense that we don't belong in our neighborhoods, countries, or cultures?

UNDERSTANDING THE TEXT

6. Where do you see Paul displaying immense humility in 3:12–13? What truths and realities motivate him to pursue Christ, grow spiritually, and progress in the faith?

7. Why is it important for Paul, in particular, to forget what "lies behind" him and instead look forward (3:13)? What "prize" does Paul look toward and strive for (3:14)?

8. What does Paul call the Philippians to do in verses 15 and 16? Why do you think Paul links maturity to a dogged pursuit of holiness and growth?

9. Paul not only points to himself as a faithful example but also uses the sinful example of others as a warning (3:17–19). What is his attitude concerning those who walk as "enemies" of Christ (v. 18)? Toward what goal and end are such people walking—and why is this tragic (v. 19)?

10. What contrast does Paul make between God's people and those who walk as enemies of Christ (3:20)? Why is the concept of true citizenship important for Christians?

11. What ultimate hope do Christians have—and what will happen when we enter our true eternal home (3:21)? What encouragement can this hope offer to believers who face suffering, discouragement, and a lack of belonging here on earth?

BIBLE CONNECTIONS

12. Read Proverbs 30:1–4, in which Agur, a man who has come to know the wisdom of God, humbly describes his own weakness, frailty, and lack of understanding. What do Agur's words tell us about his heart? Why is it important for even the most mature Christians to continue to embrace and admit their weakness, frailty, and need for growth in Christ?

Humility in Action, pg. 237
Because God's sheer grace has conferred on heaven's citizens unimaginable privileges, we are humbled, not haughty; patient, not proud; eager to serve, not demanding service; outgoing toward others, not turned in on ourselves. Heavenly-mindedness is humility in action on earth, serving, forgiving, loving others in everyday life.

13. The apostle Peter refers to Christians in ancient Asia Minor as "elect exiles" who have an inheritance that is "kept in heaven" for them (1 Peter 1:1–2, 4). What makes Peter's point reminiscent of Paul's teaching about the "citizenship" of believers? What important truths do both Paul and Peter tell us about how God's people should understand their place in this world?

THEOLOGY CONNECTIONS

14. Answer 75 of the Westminster Larger Catechism describes the process of sanctification as one in which believers "more and more die unto sin" as they follow Jesus, obey God's Word, and receive strength from the indwelling Holy Spirit. Why is it important for us to understand that, while our sanctification increases in this life, it is never finally completed or perfected?

15. Romans 13:1–7, along with other passages in Scripture, calls God's people to be good earthly citizens—to submit to governing authorities, pay taxes, and fulfill civic duties. Why should it actually make us even more faithful, respectful, and kind citizens of our earthly homes and cities when we understand that "our citizenship is in heaven" (Phil. 3:20)?

APPLYING THE TEXT

16. What does this passage imply that a *lack* of desire for ongoing spiritual growth (in the areas of obedience, love for Christ, knowledge of God's Word, and so on) might indicate about a person's spiritual maturity? How can you cultivate an attitude like the one shown by Paul, who continually pressed on to know Christ more and more?

17. Why is it important for you to remember that you have the identity of someone who belongs to Christ and is a citizen of heaven? What tends to distract you from keeping these truths in mind and leads you to pursue worldly identity and belonging?

18. How ought you to respond to immature Christians, in light of the fact that you, like Paul, are far from perfect (3:12–13)? How should you feel about those who are chasing after sin, worldly pleasure, and temporal significance (3:18–19)? In what ways can this passage serve to spur you toward a bolder and clearer witness for the gospel?

PRAYER PROMPT

Paul encourages the Philippians—and us—to keep seeking to know Christ the Savior more and more! Today, as you conclude this lesson, ask God to give you the strength and motivation, through his Spirit, to press on in your walk with him and chase after Jesus with joyful hope. Ask him to graciously remind you, especially when you are facing times of discouragement, that your true citizenship is in heaven, where you will be transformed as you enter the eternal presence of your Savior.

Know Christ as Christ Knows You, pg. 223
If you are a Christian, . . . you must share Paul's longing to become a person who responds eagerly, instinctively to God's love by loving your Redeemer "all out" and loving other people sacrificially. Resting in the mercy that he has already lavished on you should whet your appetite for more, spurring you to sprint toward the goal of knowing him as he knows you.

LESSON 11

STANDING TOGETHER

Philippians 4:1–3

THE BIG PICTURE

Paul now calls the saints in Philippi to stand firm in the Lord (4:1)—in stark contrast to those we saw in 3:18, who walk as "enemies . . . of Christ." The affection that the apostle feels in his heart for the Philippian believers is again revealed at the beginning of Philippians 4, in which he writes that he loves and longs for them and sees them as his "joy and crown" (v. 1). Paul's greatest desire for these beloved followers of Christ is that they will stand in the Lord firmly and faithfully until the end.

Yet, as we have seen already, a major threat to the Philippians' ability to stand firm in the Lord has emerged within the church: divisions and factions among its members (4:2). The entreaties that Paul has been offering now take a very personal turn as he calls out two female church members— Euodia and Syntyche—by name. The apostle commands them to "agree in the Lord" (v. 2) before turning to invite others in the church to join him in helping these women (4:3). There is some debate over the identity of the "true companion" Paul mentions in verse 3, though his reasons for calling on this person are clear: these women, who are now sinfully quarreling, previously served side by side with Paul for the sake of the gospel of Jesus Christ. Euodia and Syntyche are one in Christ and yoked together through gospel ministry, and now they must graciously forgive each other and pursue agreement and peace.

The frank and direct confrontation that we see in these verses illustrates an important aspect of gospel community and ministry: disunity can threaten even the healthiest of churches and the most vibrant communities of believers. With this concern in mind, Paul will not let these women off the hook! Instead, he commands them to pursue unity, peace, and agreement in the Lord, whom they have served together and must now worship and proclaim in loving unity.

Read Philippians 4:1–3.

GETTING STARTED

1. Describe a time that you saw disunity or relational conflict pull apart a team, staff, or group of friends. What was the emotional impact of the fracture on the members of the group? How could they have prevented such an outcome?

2. What truths, convictions, and goals should hold Christians in unity, even when they experience disagreements and relational tension? What kinds of situations *can* make it necessary for Christians to divide and separate?

Speaking the Truth in Love, pg. 243

Paul must choose his words with the utmost care. Spirit-filled apostle and pastor that he is, Paul does so with consummate tenderness and skill. His wording and tone not only reach our hearts on the issues he addresses, but also teach us much about how we ourselves can speak "the truth in love" (Eph. 4:15) when others may not wish to hear it.

OBSERVING THE TEXT

3. Read through this brief passage from Philippians several times as you prepare to study it in detail. What do you observe about the tone of these verses Paul is writing? What do they reveal about his heart and the emotional and personal connection he has with his readers?

4. Imagine if you were Euodia or Syntyche and you heard this letter being read aloud in the church in Philippi. What would be your immediate response, and why?

5. What is the basis of the appeal Paul makes for these two women to agree and be unified? Where does he direct their attention?

UNDERSTANDING THE TEXT

6. In what way do the opening words of Philippians 4 serve as fitting concluding remarks to chapter 3?

7. In 4:1, what does Paul do to ground his appeal to the Philippians in love—and what should encourage them about the way he feels and thinks about them?

8. Take a moment to go back and read Philippians 2:1–4 again. What general principle does Paul establish, there, regarding unity and humility in the church? In what way do the commands from those four verses, as well as the example of Christ's selfless humility that 2:5–11 shows us, serve as a foundation for the more personal rebuke that we see in 4:2–3?

9. What can we conclude about Euodia and Syntyche's relationship, conflict, and disagreement, based on 4:2? Since Paul is confronting them directly, what effect is their disunity potentially having on the Philippian church and the fellowship and mission that it shares?

10. What appeal does Paul make to others in the congregation alongside the rebuke and confrontation he offers to the two quarreling women (4:3)? What can we learn from this about the role that all believers in the church (and not just pastors) play in confronting, rebuking, exhorting, and encouraging one another?

11. The call Paul issues for agreement and unity is grounded in these women's past work, on behalf of the gospel, and on their future together. What do we learn from this about why believers in Christ should seek unity and agreement?

BIBLE CONNECTIONS

12. Read Psalm 133. What is the psalmist celebrating, here? What surprising metaphors and pictures does he use? What thematic connections do you see between this psalm and Philippians 4:1–3?

13. Paul's willingness to rebuke and confront members of a church is not unique to his apostolic ministry to the Philippians. Read 1 Corinthians 1:10–17. What types of divisions and disunity were threatening the church in Corinth? What seems to be at the root of the divisions that church was experiencing?

Paul Names Names, pg. 243
Paul has laid the foundation for his loving entreaty to Euodia and Syntyche in his earlier appeal to the whole congregation, "Complete my joy by being of the same mind, having the same love, being in full accord and of one mind. Do nothing from rivalry or conceit, but in humility count others more significant than yourselves" (Phil. 2:2–3). Now he approaches the problem head-on, naming names and appealing for reconciliation.

THEOLOGY CONNECTIONS

14. "Peace if possible; truth at all costs!" is a declaration attributed to the great Reformer Martin Luther. Consider the Protestant Reformation in light of Philippians 4:1–3—did it go against Paul's command? Why or why not? When we disagree with other believers, what steps can we take to determine whether it is possible to "agree in the Lord" or whether commitment to God's truth justifies a parting of the ways?

15. Does the fact that different denominations exist violate Paul's call for us to "agree" in the Lord? Why, or why not?

APPLYING THE TEXT

16. What does the appeal that Paul makes to his "true companion" teach you about the responsibility you have, as a member of the church, for calling fellow believers to seek unity, peace, and agreement in the Lord? Have you shied away from this responsibility in the past? Why, or why not?

17. Do you have broken relationships with brothers and sisters in Christ that are causing tension in the church? If so, how could you work toward agreeing with them "in the Lord" (4:2)? What do you perhaps need to repent of? What may you need to forgive, in light of the forgiveness Christ has shown you?

18. What does this passage tell us about the importance of being unified for the gospel—and specifically for the sake of the gospel's *mission*? Why should we reconcile with other believers out of not only a desire for the church's *internal peace* but also a concern for its *external witness*?

A Third Person Involved, pgs. 253–54

When your relationship with a Christian brother or sister hits an impasse, when you cannot resolve a disagreement, . . . you both need to pause and take to heart Paul's gentle reminder to Euodia and Syntyche that there is a third person involved. The tense situation includes not only believers who disagree with each other and hurt each other, but also *the Lord*, in whom you both now live as citizens of heaven.

PRAYER PROMPT

Paul's exhortation regarding unity in Philippians 4:1–3 (and his willingness to name names!) illustrates the fundamental importance of our standing "firm" in the Lord as we also stand *together* in gospel unity. Today, pray for God to draw you into joyful unity with other believers in your community. Ask him to give you a gracious and forgiving spirit when you experience tension or disagreement with others—one that allows you to work toward agreeing with them "in the Lord" for the sake of God's glory and the peace of the church.

LESSON 12

ANXIETY AND CONTENTMENT

Philippians 4:4–13

THE BIG PICTURE

There was much that the Philippian believers could worry about. Socially marginalized first-century Christians faced ridicule and scorn . . . and sometimes even persecution and danger. Add to this the Philippians' anxiety over the situation Paul faced as an old man imprisoned because of the gospel. Yet in this passage Paul calls them to embrace the joy and contentment that he himself models—a joy and contentment that cannot be touched by earthly circumstances, because they are tethered to Christ.

As he approaches the conclusion of his letter, Paul twice calls the Philippians to "rejoice" in the Lord (4:4). In light of the fact that the Lord is present with his people, Paul calls the Philippians away from anxiety and toward constant prayer and steady peace in God their Savior (4:5–7). Paul instructs these believers to direct their thoughts to God's grace and beauty before calling them again to follow the example he has set regarding all these things (4:8–9).

Next, Paul offers his own life as an example of how to have joyful contentment in every circumstance imaginable (4:10–13). He explains that he has discovered the "secret" of an unshakeable contentment in Christ that lasts throughout riches and poverty, joy and pain, suffering and delight (vv. 10–12). That secret is Jesus Christ, his Savior, through whom he can do "all" this—can remain joyful and content in every circumstance (v. 13). Thus, this well-known verse, which concludes this section, does not concern worldly accomplishment but rather promotes Christ-centered contentment—a good gift from God that is available to all who place their faith in his Son.

Read Philippians 4:4–13.

GETTING STARTED

1. What kinds of issues or circumstances tend to cause you the most worry, anxiety, and stress? Why? How often would you say you worry throughout the week? How do you respond when anxiety strikes?

2. Describe a time when you heard Philippians 4:13 being taught or applied in a way that tied it to worldly accomplishment. What does the rest of the context of chapter 4 indicate about what this verse is actually saying?

Anchored, pgs. 260–61

Paul presents a far stronger antidote to anxiety than politicians' promises, cheery self-coaching, or calming meditation. He directs his Philippian friends and us to a life-anchor that goes deeper than the surface storms of circumstances, even deeper than whatever emotional equilibrium we could muster through happy talk or mellow mantras or any other stress-management technique. Paul offers us an anchor that secures our well-being eternally in the life and love of the ever-living God.

OBSERVING THE TEXT

3. Paul gives several commands in Philippians 4:4–6. What are they? How are they related to the character, presence, and promises of God?

4. What does Philippians 4:8 tell us about our thought lives—and about our ability to shape and direct them?

5. Paul covers the gamut of human experience—both negative and positive—in Philippians 4:10–12. Think about what you know about Paul. What extreme circumstances did he experience throughout the course of his life?

UNDERSTANDING THE TEXT

6. What does Paul's repeated *command* to "rejoice" (4:4) tell us about the kind of joy he has in mind and its relation to our emotions, feelings, and moods?

7. What truths about God form the basis of Paul's command for us to reject worry (4:5–7)? What role does Paul say prayer needs to play in our battles with anxiety?

8. What does Paul call the Philippians to intentionally shape and focus their thoughts around (4:8)? Why do you think he offers himself, again, as their example (4:9)? What promise from God that we saw in 4:7 does Paul repeat in verse 9?

9. Philippians 4:10 shows us how grateful Paul is for the financial provision and support the Philippian church has been giving him. What does this verse tell us about the ways the church can partner with those who are involved in gospel ministry? Why is it important for God's people to demonstrate this kind of "concern" for fellow workers of the gospel?

God Must Be Involved, pg. 264

Paul keeps playing one tune: the antidote to anxiety is to have the living God deeply involved in your life. Whether he is addressing how to find emotional equilibrium in trouble . . . , how to respond to those who reject or resist us . . . , how to petition the Father . . . , or how to cultivate Christ-centered "habits of the heart" . . . , at every turn Paul shows us another facet of the anxiety-banishing constancy and compassion of our Creator and Redeemer.

10. What does Paul clarify, in 4:10–12, about the source and foundation of his joy? What highs and lows of the human experience does he describe in these verses?

11. What does the context of the rest of Philippians 4 show us that verse 13 means? What is it that Paul can "do" through Christ who strengthens him? Why is a contextual understanding of this verse so important? What does it promise to believers—and what is it instructing us to pursue through Christ our Savior?

BIBLE CONNECTIONS

12. Read Colossians 1:24, and skim through the surrounding verses as well, to discover the reason that Paul rejoices even when he is suffering. How, and why, can the apostle experience such joy even when he is in the midst of great pain and hardship?

13. Paul's contentment arises not only from Christ but also from the hope of future glory, treasure, and splendor that is his *through* Christ. Read 2 Corinthians 4:16–18. How can the glorious promises in this passage help you to be content as well—even as you are in the midst of changing earthly circumstances?

14. Read 2 Corinthians 8:1–5. What does this passage tell us about the Philippian Christians' circumstances? After knowing this background, what do you think was Paul's pastoral purpose for sharing his own insight into the secret of being content in Christ?

THEOLOGY CONNECTIONS

15. Answer 27 of the Westminster Shorter Catechism explains that Christ's "humiliation consisted in his being born, and that in a low condition, made under the law, undergoing the miseries of this life, the wrath of God, and the cursed death of the cross." How can remembering the "humiliation" of our Savior help us and encourage us when we are, in the words of Philippians 4:12, "brought low"?

16. William Tyndale translated the Bible into English—and was strangled to death with a chain as punishment for his offense. His last words were "Lord, open the king of England's eyes." How does William Tyndale—along with the many others who gave their lives for God's Word and the advancement of the gospel of Jesus Christ—model for us how to be content in Christ, and to hope for eternal glory, despite earthly suffering and pain?

APPLYING THE TEXT

17. What can this passage teach you about your struggle with anxiety and worry? What promises of God are you forgetting whenever you give yourself to anxiety and worry? What can you do in order to seek the peace of your God and Savior more intentionally?

18. Do you intentionally choose, shape, and focus your thoughts in the ways Paul commands in Philippians 4:8? If not, why not? How can God's Word aid you with focusing and directing your thought life in a more Christ-exalting and God-honoring way?

19. Does what Paul says about the contentment he has found, in every situation, convict your heart? What could you do to cultivate deeper contentment in Christ in response to this passage? In what ways are you tethering your joy and delight to your changing worldly circumstances? How could you instead tether your joy to Christ your Savior and the eternal glory you hope for in him?

PRAYER PROMPT

Paul's contentment in Christ springs from his own experiences with the full range and extremes of human circumstances. He knew wealth and success; he also knew intense poverty and ridicule. He knew honor and shame, fame and suffering. The apostle calls God's people to fight for the same contentment in Christ to which he clung throughout his life. Today, ask your God to remind you of the treasure and eternal riches that you have in Jesus, and pray for the strength to fight for the same contentment that Paul had as you too tether your joy to Christ your Savior!

The Fight for Contentment, pg. 295

Christian contentment is something that we fight for. We must exert effort to wage war against the temptation to complain, to envy others, to fixate on what is uncomfortable and inconvenient and downright wrong in our circumstances. We strive to focus instead on the faithfulness and mercy and strength of our God. Paul flexes his mental muscle to remind himself often that in Christ he already has the supreme treasure, and that he is racing toward a goal that will mean an even greater experience of his Savior's grace and glory.

LESSON 13

GETTING BY GIVING

Philippians 4:14–23

THE BIG PICTURE

Paul's letter to the Philippians draws to a close with another reminder of the sweet gospel partnership that the elderly apostle and the church in Philippi shared. Paul had been instrumental in leading some of the first Philippian believers to Christ and establishing their church, and in turn the church had supported his ministry financially—even from a distance. In this lesson, we will see Paul celebrate the generosity of the Philippian church and rejoice in the spiritual blessings these believers receive when they share in his gospel ministry for the sake of Jesus Christ.

Paul writes, first, of the Philippian church's generous and continued support—support that stands out from that of many of the other churches he has helped to lead and plant (4:14–16). As before, though, Paul is clear that his gratitude for the Philippians' financial support does not flow from anxiety or discontent; he rejoices in their provision for him, which will ultimately bring spiritual "fruit that increases" to their "credit" in Christ (4:17). Their gift is not ultimately about Paul; it is actually a "fragrant offering" and "sacrifice" to God that is pleasing to him (4:18). After rejoicing in the spiritual benefit that the Philippians' generosity has brought them, the apostle voices his confident expectation that God will continue to supply their needs in Christ—and all to the glory of his name (4:19–20).

Paul concludes his letter with words of blessing and grace, and he conveys greetings from the saints in "Caesar's household" (4:21–23). His relationship with saints in Rome provides yet another glimpse of his mission: to be a gospel witness in every circumstance . . . including imprisonment.

Read Philippians 4:14–23.

GETTING STARTED

1. Has *giving* a gift ever brought you more joy than *receiving* one? If so, describe that experience. What did you learn from it?

2. Think about how you have heard Christian leaders, churches, and ministries talk about money and finances. Some may hesitate to say anything about money; others may constantly talk about their financial status or need. What leader or ministry has handled this issue well, in your opinion? What principles are important for the area of communicating about finances for ministry?

Riches in Glory, pg. 312

The grace of the Lord Jesus Christ is just the note that [Paul] wants to leave ringing in his friends' ears and hearts! God's riches in glory are opened to us in Christ Jesus. They flow into our lives, free of charge, because the beloved Son paid the price to erase our debt to God's justice and to usher us into the family, to share his inheritance with us.

OBSERVING THE TEXT

3. As this passage begins, in 4:14–16, what might lead us to think that Paul is about to ask for *more* support from the Philippians—or at least to indicate his dependency on them?

4. Are you surprised by the shift in Paul's tone and focus that is introduced in 4:17–19? What does he focus on as he discusses the financial support the Philippian believers have given him? Does he mention anything about his ongoing financial need?

5. What initial observations do you have about the final words of greeting Paul shares in 4:21–23? Which group of saints does he mention specifically—and what does this tell us?

UNDERSTANDING THE TEXT

6. The generous support that the church in Philippi provided to Paul was evidently noteworthy and distinguished them from other churches— how does Paul call attention to this in 4:14–16?

7. Although he appreciates their financial contributions to his ministry, Paul ultimately seeks something *for* the Philippians rather than *from* them (4:17). What is it?

8. How does Paul describe the gift that the Philippians sent him—and how does this description demonstrate that his focus is fundamentally on their worship and relationship with God (4:18)?

9. What does Paul promise the Philippian believers in 4:19–20? Will the Philippians receive earthly health or riches because of the generosity they have shown him? If not, what will they receive instead (v. 19)?

10. In 4:21–22, what do we learn about the community Paul has with other believers? What is surprising about the connections he has made?

11. What do you think the Philippian believers would find encouraging about Paul's closing words (4:21–23)? How do these words serve to call them, again, to forsake anxiety and instead to find joy and comfort in the Lord and in the advancement of the gospel?

BIBLE CONNECTIONS

12. Read Acts 17:1–9, in which Luke describes Paul's tumultuous visit to Thessalonica. Why does it seem Paul would have needed financial help and support during this visit? Why do you think he specifically notes, in Philippians 4:16, that the Philippians helped him during this particular point in his ministry?

13. The theme of getting by giving—of the greater blessing that comes through giving than through receiving—is one that the apostle Paul develops more than once. Read 2 Corinthians 9:6–11. What blessings does it promise to those who give generously and cheerfully? What themes and ideas from this passage overlap with those from Philippians 4:14–20?

Partners in Giving, pg. 297

Despite the Philippians' "extreme poverty" (as Paul characterized it in 2 Cor. 8:2), their financial support for Paul's gospel mission was outstanding for its consistency and its generosity. Paul recalls that when he left Macedonia, heading south to Achaian cities such as Athens and Corinth, the Philippian Christians promptly sent a gift as his partners "in giving and receiving" (Phil. 4:15).

THEOLOGY CONNECTIONS

14. The "health and wealth" gospel—or "prosperity" gospel—is a false teaching that links obedience, faithfulness, and generosity with physical health or financial prosperity (or both!). What makes this false teaching dangerous? Based on your study of this epistle, and of this passage in particular, how could you demonstrate that this is *not* a teaching promoted by Paul?

15. The Westminster Confession of Faith reminds us that Jesus "purchased, not only reconciliation, but an everlasting inheritance in the kingdom of heaven, for all those whom the Father has given unto him" (8.5). What does this imply about the nature of the "riches" that Paul promises God will supply to the Philippians (4:19)?

APPLYING THE TEXT

16. Are you contributing financially to the growth of the gospel, both locally and globally? What sacrifices should you perhaps make in order to increase your giving? Why is supporting gospel ministry an important part of Christian life and discipleship?

17. What spiritual blessings do people risk missing out on when they hold back from being financially generous? Why is it so important to remember that Paul does not promise physical health or worldly wealth to the Philippians because of their financial support?

18. How can the gospel witness that Paul engaged in, and the success that he evidently experienced—even among, as we saw earlier, "the whole imperial guard" (1:13) and perhaps, now, even "Caesar's household" (4:22)—serve to encourage you? With whom might you share the good news of the salvation that's available through Jesus Christ—and what could you do to make sure this happens even this week?

The Transformation of Giving, pg. 302

[Paul's] perspective transforms giving toward missions from duty or charity into privilege and joy. You get to give your hard-earned dollars for missions not only because your missionaries need the funds, but also because the living God has brought you into partnership with himself, and through your giving you can bring glory "to our God and Father . . . forever and ever" (Phil. 4:20).

PRAYER PROMPT

The gratitude Paul expresses for the Philippian believers' financial generosity arises more from his joy over their spiritual blessing than from the financial provision he has received from them. What a good reminder for us as we pursue gospel-centered generosity! Today, pray that God would open your heart to see how you can support the work of his kingdom—both in your local church and around the world. Ask him to help you to lay down your life, and open your hands, in generous service for the gospel until Jesus comes again—and to you remind you of what a spiritual blessing it is to do so.

Jon Nielson is senior pastor of Spring Valley Presbyterian Church in Roselle, Illinois, and the author of *Bible Study: A Student's Guide*, among other books. He has served in pastoral positions at Holy Trinity Church, Chicago, and College Church, Wheaton, Illinois, and as director of training for the Charles Simeon Trust.

Dennis E. Johnson (ThM, Westminster Theological Seminary; PhD, Fuller Theological Seminary) taught New Testament and practical theology at Westminster Seminary California for nearly four decades. An ordained minister, he is the author of several books and commentaries, including *Him We Proclaim* and *Triumph of the Lamb*, and a contributor to several more.

P&R PUBLISHING'S COMPANION COMMENTARY

Philippians is a magisterial treatment of crucial topics that Paul relates to the touchstone of Christ, his cross, and his resurrection. Johnson shows how Paul, writing from prison to a church close to his heart, uses his own experience and attitude as exemplars to show the Philippians the difference a Christ-formed mind makes to the way believers respond to adversity, rivalry, conflict, vanity, and achievement; pursue holiness; and strategically deploy resources for the gospel.

The Reformed Expository Commentary (REC) series is accessible to both pastors and lay readers. Each volume in the series provides exposition that gives careful attention to the biblical text, is doctrinally Reformed, focuses on Christ through the lens of redemptive history, and applies the Bible to our contemporary setting.

Praise for the Reformed Expository Commentary Series

"Well-researched and well-reasoned, practical and pastoral, shrewd, solid, and searching." —**J. I. Packer**

"A rare combination of biblical insight, theological substance, and pastoral application." —**Al Mohler**

"Here, rigorous expository methodology, nuanced biblical theology, and pastoral passion combine." —**R. Kent Hughes**